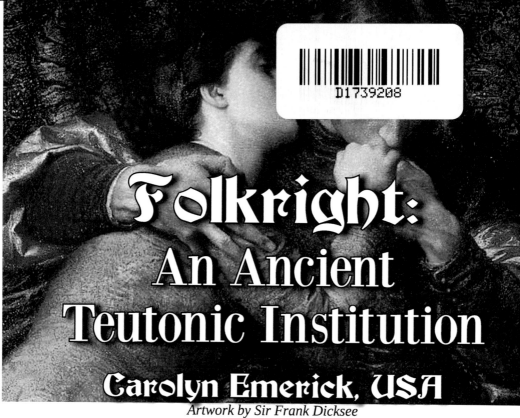

Folkright: An Ancient Teutonic Institution

Carolyn Emerick, USA

Artwork by Sir Frank Dicksee

The world finds itself today at a fork in the road. We can take the path toward globalism which uses cultural Marxism to subdue the masses into a lobotomized march toward ethnic homogenization, or we can assert our right to exist as unique ethno-cultures and demand the ability to preserve and protect that which makes us unique. Ultimately, globalism will destroy all world cultures, so the impetus to double down on cultural identity is in no way a "racist" impulse. However, these rootless international elites have long been burrowed within the societies of the West. Ergo, Western culture is simultaneously their guinea pig, their first victim, as well as their launch pad to spread outward into the wider world. Thus, ethnic-Europeans are among the first in the world to wake up to the threat that these entities pose. This realization is coupled with the understanding that we are the prime-target and most at risk of losing ourselves in the immediate. But, because we are the first to feel the pinch and speak out for our survival, our enemies hurl accusations of "supremacy" at us in an attempt to undermine our struggle via means that come directly from Saul Alinsky's famous "Rules for Radicals," the handbook for cultural subterfuge. While many are waking up to this reality, too many who believe they understand the situation are oblivious to just how long this has been underway. Indigenous European culture has, indeed, been under direct onslaught for centuries. If we are engaging in a rescue mission to save ourselves, it is all for naught if we fail to be informed by our own indigenous cultural customs and ancient worldview.

Anglo-Saxon Tribal Culture

Anglo-Saxon culture is greatly misrepresented when described as a "Christian" one, even after nominal conversion. Many scholars of the period have described the "conversion" process as more of a "Germanization" of Christianity rather than a "Christianization" of these Germanic people. Indeed, the notion that the Anglo-Saxons were "Christian" in the way that we consider the meaning of the term today is utterly preposterous when one looks at what was going on in Anglo-Saxon England with any semblance of objectivity. What we find in "Christian" Anglo-Saxon England is a society wherein ancient pagan fertility rites were still being enacted by both the public and the "church" clergy, and supposedly "Christian" earls and other nobility were still swearing oaths by "the Thunderer." Most importantly for our discussion is that the Anglo-Saxons were still operating under the old Indo-European (Aryan) mode of tribal social structure.

The Aryans seeded cultures in Europe, India, and Persia. They can be broken down into the Indo-European and Indo-Iranian branches. The Indo-Europeans then sub-divided into the majority of linguisto-cultural groups we know in Europe today; i.e. Germanic, Celtic, Slavic, etc. Indo-European culture was markedly different than the kind of society that was ushered in after the Christian invasion and subversion of European society. Aryan society was not classless. In fact, we had a society with a caste system not unlike the Hindu *varna* system. However, the roles and position of the commoner versus the

Artwork by Edmund Blair Leighton

nobility was strikingly different than what we imagine. Our view of aristocracy and peasantry is informed by the Christian feudal system, which was literally the upending of traditional European worldview and the enslavement of Europeans. The Indo-Europeans operated under what has been termed a "tripartite" caste system. In reality, there were four classes: the slaves, the freemen, the nobility, and the king-priest class. There was some level of social mobility, but particulars vary by each sub-culture. The class we are particularly interested for this discussion is the freeman class.

Christianity did not properly saturate Europe until indigenous Europeans were conquered and enslaved into the feudal system. The Christian ideology was essentially a brainwashing tool to enforce submission to this new system. Although the history books will say that the Anglo-Saxons were "Christian" at the time of the Norman Invasion, the truth of the matter is that they were operating under an Aryan-Teutonic tribal social structure, still engaging in pagan practices, the gods of their ancestors were still prevalent within their cultural milieu; and significantly, the Anglo-Saxons fought under the traditional dragon banner whilst the conquering Normans fought under the flag of the cross. The reason that Saint George was subsequently named the patron saint of England is because it is literally the story of the "cross" slaying the "dragon." In other words, St. George's cross, the modern flag of England today, celebrates the enslavement of the English people. The Normans were notorious castle builders. What modern tourists often forget is that these castles were not built for any fairytale-inspired whimsy, but they were used logistically to enforce the new feudal system and keep the Anglo-Saxons under the thumb of their new Norman over-lords. But, crucially, people also forget that the same figures who built those castles also built the cathedrals – and for the same purpose.

Folkright and Teutonic Society

Folkright was a cultural norm embedded into Anglo-Saxon law, essentially the Old English "common law," with roots in ancient Teutonic tribal society. Teutonic culture, although there were variations depending on the specific tribe and the time period, generally followed the typical Aryan caste system. The general class of freemen were the "*karl*" class, the Anglo-Saxon linguistic variant being called "*ceorl.*" Under Anglo-Saxon law, the rights of free men (and women) were enshrined in a cultural institution known as "folkright," (*folcriht*). The system of folkright ensured that the nobility's power did not allow for tyranny and that all free men were guaranteed "unalienable" rights under the protection of the law. (There is reason to view the American founding fathers' intention as an attempt to revive ancient Teutonic society based on Old English common law). Dictionary.com defines "folkright" as "a law or right of the people as opposed to that of the privileged classes," and Merriam Webster says, "the right of the people under the customary laws and usages especially in early England." Germanic society has been called "egalitarian" by some scholars in comparison to the Christian feudalism that would ensue. In truth, it was not without class structure and hierarchy. But, the rights of freemen were considered unalienable and it protected all freemen (which also meant women) under the rule of law. "Encyclopedia of European Peoples" says that "folkright" granted free commoners "many personal rights" such as "his right to bear arms, to attend and air grievances at local courts." It continues on, "folkright consisted of the collective will of the people as embodied in rules and laws that had been established over time." It also says that "the relationship between king and commoner bypassed coercive power wielded by local lords." This is an allusion to the old Aryan concept of sacral kingship.

While Aryan society did maintain a caste system, as we can see, not only were the rights of the commoner enshrined in law and cultural custom, but the king-class was duty-bound to the commoners who made up the bulk of society. This system meant that nobility did not operate on the basis of wealth and a superiority of privilege that can easily result in tyranny. The "regular Joe" was protected under the law and the highest office in the land had

obligations to his tribesmen, just as the freemen were obligated to their king. Feudalism went hand in hand with Christendom. It was a system that held contempt for the old mores of honor and rights of all men and women. Interestingly, the word "churl," most commonly known from Shakespearean speech as a derogatory term for a low-born peasant, is actually derived from the Anglo-Saxon "ceorl," meaning the "karl," or freeman, caste. So, we can see that under the Norman-Christian feudal system, the common man became an object of contempt for the ruling class.

In a book called "The Constitutional History of Medieval England: From the English Settlement to 1485," published in 1937, scholar J.E.A. Jolliffe, discusses how "folkright" was intermingled with tribal notions of "blood-ties." Just as the king was obligated to the freemen of the tribe, the larger tribe was, itself, made up of a network of kinship. He says that this kind of society *"throws the whole weight of habit against the forces of free economy and individualism, and ignores landed or other wealth as a* criterion of rank or authority. Not until the exclusive reverence for descent has been sapped by centuries of economic and political experience, is the way clear for the rudiments of feudalism and the territorial state," (p5). Essentially, this kind of kinship-based tribal society with fundamental rights of free-men had to be eradicated to make way for Christian feudal enslavement. He continues,

"From the assumed community of descent a common inheritance of law was deduced. Law was an attribute of the stock, and every member of it was born into folkright, a complex of privilege, status, and obligation coming to him with his father's blood and his material inheritance of land and goods. Such a man was said to be folk-free… Ideally, in the theory of society held by the northern world as a whole, folkright endowed the individual with all that was necessary for the completeness of life --a sufficiency of land equal in amount among equals in rank, and the status of his immediate ancestors, noble, free, or half-free. An equal law gave him a sure process of defence in folkmoots, where his landright and his person were defended by common right, and by judgment of his neighbours."

If this sounds utopian, it is important to understand that this is the worldview we European folk lived by under our indigenous ethnos. The loss of such a worldview owes its demise directly to Christianity

Artwork by Edmund Blair Leighton

thrust upon us from the new elite class for the purpose of our own enslavement. To understand how closely linked the Christian church was with this new form of government, it is helpful to look at a book called "Feudal Germany," by James Westfall Thompson, 1928. He explains:

"In the Middle Ages the church was much more than a religious institution. It was a political, civil, social, economic institution of portentous power and of vast dimension. Its proprietary nature involved it in the network of the feudal régime to a degree which requires some effort of historical imagination to realize. Bishops and abbots were feudal lords, and the machinery of the church was intricately interwoven with the machinery of feudal government," (p3).

Though Thompson is speaking about the Carolingian dynasty on the European continent a few centuries prior to the Norman Invasion, it is important to note that he is describing the same system. William the Bastard brought feudalism into Britain after it had been firmly established upon the European continent and simply continued on with the suppression of the indigenous Teutonic way of life. He continues:

"In the tumultuous laboratory of the ninth century the old order of things was broken up and a new civilization came out of the crucible. Feudalism emerged as a complete political, economic, and social polity, and the feudal states of France, Germany, and Italy came into being," (p5).

Well, he is describing the destruction of the Aryan way of life and forced subjugation of the European people under Christian feudalism. Thompson continues on to explain that although Charlemagne's dynasty had attempted to control the church, very quickly, the church was in control of the state:

"With the break-up of the Carolingian empire in the ninth century, the relations of state and church began to be reversed. Hitherto the state had controlled the church. Now the church began to control the state. The amalgamation of church and state became more complete than before, and the church saw to it that it was well repaid for its services to the government," (p5).

The establishment of the church intertwined with government was also intimately connected with the establishment of the banking system as we know it (see: "Elite-Driven Social Engineering and the Norman Conquest,"p33). Thus, the new "elites," the church, and the monetary system were working in sync with one another. The feudal enslavement of Europeans was a system by which the nobility enriched themselves off of the work of serfs, who were not much better off than slaves. There was no longer a system of protection of the rights of freemen against the tyranny of the nobility. This is whence the modern idea of aristocracy versus peasantry derives. Prior to Christian feudalism, to be a "ceorl" would have been a point of the pride of being among the free class which was imbued with rights and protection under the law. With the instatement of Christian feudalism, the term evolved to the insult we are more familiar with, "churl." One can almost see the snarling grin of our overlords as they hurl our ancient Aryan caste title at us with a sneer as they spit upon the ground toiled on by our ancestors.

Artwork by Edmund Blair Leighton

We Need Our Druids

When we look at the events in the world today, more and more people are waking up to the realization that something is terribly wrong. But, as we continue to live as economic slaves to the system we are locked into, most people are too absorbed in the weekly grind to give their time, energy, and attention to the kind of deep study it entails to fully grasp what is going on, who is behind it, and just how long it has been happening. As mentioned at the outset of this discussion, Aryan society maintained a caste system – but one wherein the upper echelons were as oathed and obligated to the commoners as the commoners were to the upper castes. Each caste performed a duty to their folk in an honor-based tribal mentality. The priest tier was known to the Celts as the *Druids* and to the Hindus as the *Brahmins*. Teutonic society surely had an equivalent, or several roles which fell within that class tier. It is important to remember that in this context, the "priest" class denotes scholars and bards as much as religious teachers. When our society was usurped, this class was the first to be targeted for complete annihilation. A restoration of our true *ethnos* would mean a complete overhaul in worldview and economic system that reinstates our ancient institution of folkright.

But, the common freeman, still enslaved by the elite banking system, cannot be relied upon or expected to put in the kind of time and study necessary to teach himself, let alone the masses, about our indigenous culture. No, for this we do need our own Druid-Brahmin tier to arise once again. Unfortunately, systems have long been in place to stop the *ceorls* from seeking their own authentic folkways. Christianity and its cousins (liberalism, cultural Marxism, and Americanisms like Mormonism, etc.) are ideologies used keep the *ceorls* in a mind-cage of psychological conditioning designed to keep the freeman in a state that is not free. It is exactly the scenario described in Plato's "Parable of the Cave," wherein a person of great learning comes with a torch to lead the enslaved cave-dwellers into the light – but they cannot accept that reality is other than the shadows they have been watching dance on the wall of the cave.

Folkright was once our unalienable right. The only thing keeping us from restoring our status as Teutonic free-folk is our stubborn refusal to leave the cave. Aryanism is in our blood. Teachers are amongst us to guide us back home again. Our own Druid-Brahmin "upper-caste" were not the "elites" who spat on us as they sneered "churl" as an insult upon the formerly free man. No, those were aristocrats handed their position of power directly by Christian feudalism and the banking monstrosity it established. And, this system still pulls the strings today. Bring back the Teutonic *Gothi* and *Gythja* (priest/priestess) and allow them to guide us back to our own indigenous *ethnos* built around the blood-ties of kith, kin, clan, and tribe – and restore the folkright to its rightful place. Let the folkright never be taken from us again!

Bibliography:

Dumezil, Georges. Mithra-Varuna. New York: Zone Books, 1988.

Goodson, Stephen. "The Hidden Origins of the Bank of England." The Barnes Review XVIII.5 (2012): 5-14.

Herbert, Kathleen. Looking for the Lost Gods of England. Anglo-Saxon Books, 1994. print.

Jolliffe, J. E. A. The Constitutional History of Medieval England: From the English Settlement to 1485. London: Adam and Charles Black, 1937. print.

Jolly, Karen Louis. Popular Religion in Late Saxon England. Chapel Hill: The University of North Carolina Press, 1996. Print.

Mason, Carl Waldman and Catherine. "Folkright." Encyclopedia of European Peoples (Regional History on File). NY: Facts on File, 2006. 321. print.

Thompson, James Westfall. Feudal Germany. Chicago: University of Chicago Press, 1928. print.

Artwork by Arthur Hughes

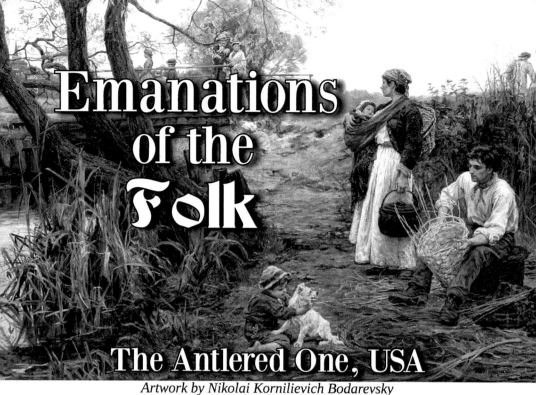

Emanations of the Folk

The Antlered One, USA

Artwork by Nikolai Kornilievich Bodarevsky

People are lost these days. We've lost anything to hold onto while simultaneously devaluing and discarding most of our identity and culture. People I care about are wandering into other damaged souls, intensifying each other's pain while soothing their loneliness. Every other person is either in therapy or lacking the ability to strive for anything at all. Are any of us content? No, we are not content; *resigned* is a better word. I see many around me resigned to a fate of mediocrity: paths not taken and places never gone because they were more comfortable in stasis. Though, they are not comfortable in a way most would think of the meaning of that word. Not cuddling with your pooch by the fire with a glass of warm tea and a rather over-sized quilt. No, they are comfortable because they are *numb*. They are numb to themselves and those around them - at least as far as I can see. They've let their aspirations become pipe-dreams because they never started the quest for that which they seek.

I am no better. I have started no journeys, made no inroads toward my destination. I have, until this point, been content to dream my dreams.

Everyone's a hero to themselves as long as they don't have to earn it. Thus, I retreated into escapism. Science fiction and action stories seemed more than enough for me. But, I was numb. And, I still am in many ways numb. Though that is changing fast. I had filled my days with a series of banalities. I lacked meaning and like many families today, I lacked self. My family was a mix of personalities: the musician, the artist, the bad boy, the black sheep, the grouch, etc. There was no ancestral story or history to my family, as much, if not all, of our genealogy was lost to time. We were more like an assortment of pieces than a unit. Like many families today, we still are fragmented.

There is a way forward for me now, though. I have found meaning in the myth, culture, and history of my own ethnic heritage. Whereas before, along with those around me, I abided almost entirely off the pop culture of our age; now I have a path to follow and now I have a history. That is what Folkism is, it is the part of me, of us, that we have dropped and can pick up again if we choose. It is the piece of us that was built maintained and treasured by generations that came before us, and that we can nurture, treasure and build onto for ourselves and all our folk to come. It is not a singular or solipsistic thing; it is the sum of a people expressed outwardly and held inward. The Hindus have this. The Amerindians have it, the Japanese have it. And, I have learned, so do we. Those of European descent in our homelands and in the diaspora - *we have a folk.*

We *are* a folk. Or, more accurately, we are many folks connected by bonds of kinship. It is demonstrated through our very speech, from our languages to the little inflections we make. It comes out in something as simple as a peasant's stew or a folksong. It resides in our myths of Odin, Zeus, Lugh, Perun, and all our heroes and gods. It finds its home in a song composed centuries ago and in the new lyrics our folk write from our hearts every day. It is all the hurt we have faced and all the triumphs and discoveries we've made. It is in our ballads, our sonnets, our novels, and our speeches. It is the art in the museums and the museums themselves, our philosophers, and our curious little ones. It is who and what we are, emanating from us and out into the world.

This is a rather vague description I know. It is hard to describe our folk in tangible terms. Not because it is unidentifiable or something unable to be understood, rather because to list all the things that make up a folk would take all the time I have left on this earth and someone to start where I stopped. I've only begun digging into my folk. I have found more meaning in Wotan than I ever found in my family's Christian faith. I have a people to research from the Germanic and Celtic tribes all the way to now and whatever fills in the time before. As well as what is made after I put these words to page.

Succinctly put, Folkism is the part of us missing that we are trying to fill. We lost our origins, our history, our culture, our names, and much more. We can find them again, they are still there. Then, forward we march, building on those who came before for those who will come after. For the Folk does not end with us; it continues on passing down that emanation as an inheritance to the next generation and the generation after that complete with an understanding of who we are, where we come from, and what that means. I've only started digging and absorbing, and I hope many more will embark on this journey of self-discovery.

Artwork by Frans Arnold Breuhaus de Groot

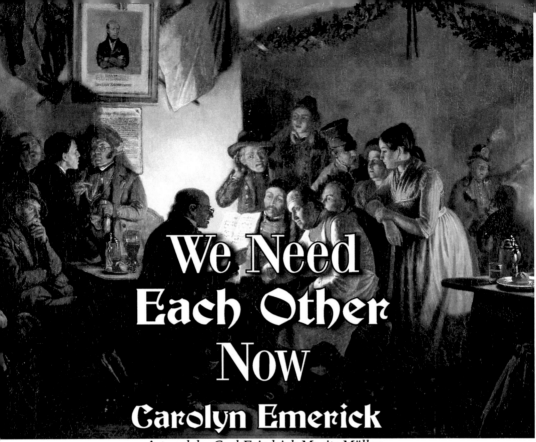

We Need Each Other Now

Carolyn Emerick

Artwork by Carl Friedrich Moritz Müller

I recently watched a documentary series made for Irish television that triggered some thoughts. Simply titled "Class Swap," the series was not politicized at all, one way or the other. It was simply a look at the Irish public school system at one high school that was participating in an exchange program with other schools throughout Europe. A handful of Irish students and teachers traveled to spend two weeks abroad to observe how other European schools operated. Despite zero effort on the part of the producers to discuss anything remotely controversial, I could not help but take note of some interesting points. The teens went to Finland, Poland, and Spain. At every school, the Irish students were welcomed by the host schools with an assembly that highlighted their own culture. The Irish teens, in return, sang songs, performed Irish dance, or otherwise demonstrated their own culture in return.

In every instance, the Irish students marveled at how

different the other European school experience was to theirs at home. Spanish students embracing for deep-throat tonsil hockey in public, they said, would not go over well in the more conservative Ireland. The Polish schools were funded and operated at the local level, with the national government paying only the teacher's salaries. This meant that there could be wide variation in how schools functioned across the nation. Still, Polish students are among the top performing in Europe. This also made the local mayor an active participant in the local school, as his own government is responsible for the school's operation.

The particular Polish school visited included all grade levels from preschool to high school. It seemed that by not separating the ages, the older students were forced to measure their own maturity level to a greater degree and understand their responsibility as role models and carers for the younger children. It also allowed for sibling groups to stay at the same school together, meaning they can look out for one another. The Finnish education system has been much discussed worldwide for its unconventional approach that yields marvelous results. The Irish teens were shocked at the casual nature of the school. Students addressed teachers by first name, could leave class early if they wished, and generally had much more freedom than the Irish students were accustomed to.

The first thing that popped out at me while watching this series was that the students themselves noted just how *different* each other European country was compared to their own. This is important in an age when non-European individuals are shoving the word "diversity" under our noses in the West and insisting that we do not have enough of it. Each one of these countries not only possesses its own language, but many regional dialects as well. The students in each of these nations were proud to share elements of their culture like traditional dress, foods, music, and even sports with their new friends.

But, the exchange experience also demonstrated that many elements of the cultures are only possible because these nations still possess the kind of cultural cohesion fomented in nations that maintain demographic integrity – that is to say, they keep their own people as the overwhelming majority. The preschoolers and younger kids toddling about in the same building as teenagers would quickly change from a tender and maturing experience to a dangerous one if the teenagers present were not raised with the same cultural norms, behaviors, and morality as the indigenous people. In the Finnish schools, the kind of lackadaisical approach taken there could never work with individuals who are not raised with the same values of independent responsibility and personal drive for achievement.

It was interesting that the school with the most non-indigenous-to-Europe "diversity" was Spain. And this was also the school that shocked the conservative Irish teens by the fragrant display of sexuality. The Spanish high school was more reminiscent of what is commonly seen in American schools; an ethnic hodge-podge and teenagers slumping around without any sense of propriety. The Finns and Poles visited were more like the home town that the Irish teens hailed from, which was more ethnically homogeneous. And in those environments, the kids all self-possessed a sense of how to behave in ways that were acceptable within their own culture.

The show got me thinking about the concept of culture and identity in the wider world today. These students were thrilled to experience new things. Indeed, the reason we travel is to experience other cultures all the world wide. Certainly, we can learn from other people. But, we must do so in a way that does not allow us to lose ourselves. We can experience other world cultures and allow them to experience ours – but this in no way should imply some kind of free-for-all. Certainly, foreigners who do not respect our own values and morals should not be made welcome in our homelands any more than we would expect to be free to disrespect their's when guests in their lands.

Another thought that came to mind while observing this cultural exchange was that ethnic-Europeans have much to teach and share amongst ourselves. Indeed, while these raving lunatics have been maniacally screeching that we need "diversity," their blatant hate for ethnic-European culture has caused us to forget about the diversity that we already possess within our own race. The globalist machine threatens each and every one of us. So, we do need to double down on reviving the impetus to cherish ourselves once again.

The irony of it is that globalism and international instantaneous communications can also allow ethnic-Europeans to connect with each other worldwide. Without this advantage, the Enemy would much more easily be able to continue to shape and mold our minds via indoctrination. But, because we now can cheaply and instantly view foreign television series such as the one discussed here, because we can reach across oceans and befriend one another via the internet, and establish real relationships due to marvels of communication technology today, we are able to transmit ideas and information to a greater degree than ever before. This means that they cannot as easily control the information,

thereby meaning they have less control over our very thoughts.

The other irony is that while we must stand firm on our own unique cultures, technology and communications allow us to look at each other and learn from one another. I am quite vocal with my criticisms of my own country. Here in America, we have failed to maintain the ethnic cohesion we once held. They have spoon-fed us the "melting pot dream" until it became a self-fulfilling nightmare. The lack of cultural identity has left a gaping hole that is plugged up by surrogates such as vapid consumerism and/or evangelical universalism. Yet, while noting these concerns, my American upbringing taught me that I have a right to self-defense, a right to bear arms, and right to speak my mind freely. These rights become ever more eroded as time marches forward. And, these are rights that my ethnic-European brethren worldwide should take note of and demand for themselves. In some Western nations, our brethren speak their thoughts at their own peril while their governments march them ever closer to a "melting pot" culture-destroying scenario. We in America can learn from our European brothers and sisters who still maintain vibrant and *authentic culture*, and they can learn from us to raise their voices *in defense of it*.

We stand right now upon a precipice wherein our fate swings in the balance between cultural renewal or utter oblivion. But, there is good news. We have not awoken too late! And, the silver lining is that more and more of us wake up every day. One voice may not be heard above the noise of the multitudes. But, there are *many* of us speaking now. Soon, our voices will become a *mighty roar* that will send our Enemy running in fear! And, let me tell you something. Anyone working this hard to annihilate a people *should* be made to quake in their boots. The Enemy is not at the gates, he is in our home. But, we're still breathing and we can save ourselves, still. All we must do is wake up and realize that we *do* have something worth saving! Right now, ethnic-Europeans who love their own culture are waking up and reaching out to our cousins around the world. We are creating such a mighty chain that they will never be able to break us! We *need* each other now. And, my heart fills with pride to see that so many of us recognize this. If we can give one another support, strength, courage, and motivation, then we are going to be just fine. Hold your head up, breathe deep, and know that this war is far from over and we can do this. We *will* survive.

Artwork by Knud Bergslien

Folkism Is for All People

Dhruba Pal, India

Artwork by Warwick Goble

The root word *Folk* has its origin from Proto-Germanic *Fulka*, Old Saxon *Folc*, Old Frisian *Folk*, Middle Dutch *Volc*, Dutch *Volk*, Old High German *Folc*, German *Volk* - all of which denotes men, people, nation, tribe. Similarly in Slavic culture, word for Folk is *Nah-Rod,* while Hindus use word *Lok* for tribe, people. So, the term "Folkism" basically depicts the lifestyle, mentality, and belief system of a folk or tribe. This is a key and integral part of any tribe as it sets out their unique identity in this world. This same concept of Folkism can also be seen in South Asia where *Sanatanis* (umbrella term for Hinduism, Buddhism, Sikhism and Jainism) believe in *Sanatan*

Dharma which basically means "Eternal Way of Life." Just like Folkism, Sanatan Dharma has a deep presence in a person's day to day life.

This can be illustrated by understanding the deep cultural presence in sports like Sumo Wrestling of Japan. The sport has Shinto (the folkish faith of Japan) origins which can be traced back through centuries. Many of the current Sumo rituals are directly related to Shinto rituals, and Sumo is also seen as bulwark of Japanese tradition. Similarly, Khusti (wrestling) in India follows a similar pattern of merging culture with sports. All the wrestlers who practice in an Akhara (traditional Indian gym) for wrestling are followers of *Bajrang Bali* (the god, Hanuman) who is a symbol of strength and undying loyalty to Dharma. These wrestlers are closely attached to Hinduism because of practices which are prevalent in *Akhara* that have strong ties with Hindu philosophy. This is also the reason why you won't find many Muslims or Christians (who are disconnected from the folkish culture of India) training in this traditional *Akhar*. At the end of the day even if any Muslim or Christian is involved with wrestling, he can't completely overlook the Hindu traditions attached with it. More importantly, both in Shinto tradition and *Sanatan Dharma* tradition, concepts like nationalism and ethnic identity are ingrained in its day to day affairs. These features are found in folkish communities all over the world along with other aspects such as a positive approach towards environment, respect for other communities as "peace'"and "harmony" are the core mottos of the creed.

However, this doesn't mean that a folkish community can't protect itself from a violent threat. Every folkish community has its own indigenous warfare style, philosophy, gods, rituals, etc., related to self defense which they resort to when it is needed to defend themselves against any threat. This resonates perfectly from the following lines where self defense and fighting for what's right is explained in great detail in *Baghvad Gita*:

Ahimsa Paramo Dharma; Dharma himsa tathaiva cha : Non-violence is the ultimate Dharma. So too is violence in service of Dharma.

In the past, Christianity and Islam have brought danger to the folkish way of life, be it in Asia or Europe. People true to their folk have stood strong against these invading forces. Even though some surrendered to the enemy, many continued their fight and even accepted death instead of being converted to their enemy's ranks. A similar practice of embracing death before dishonor is seen in Japanese culture where the Samurai used to perform *Seppuku* so as to die with honor and not be tortured and humiliated by the enemy. In India, Hindu *Rajput* women used to commit *Jauhar* which is

Artwork by Warwick Goble

committing suicide by jumping into a fire, as it's a far better option than becoming a sex slave under Muslim rulers and being humiliated for life. The best example of folkish resistance to Abrahamic aggression in Europe comes from "The Battle of Saule," where the folkish (pagan) Samogitians defeated a powerful adversary who was forcefully converting the Baltic tribes to Christianity. Just like Europe, Bharat (the folkish name of India) too had empires like the Maratha Hindu Empire, Sikh Empire, Ahoms of Assam, Hindu Rajput Kingdoms, etc., who all fought against Islamic invaders in order to protect their culture from being annihilated and erased forever.

The very reason why our forefathers preferred death rather than converting is because in every folkish culture there is a freedom in exploring yourself and reaching to one's zenith. The freedom folkish culture gives to a man is something that Abrahamic ideology cannot give because their ultimate aim is controlling the human psyche and mentality for the benefits of those in power. This particular thing was understood by our ancestors. Also, in every folkish culture you will find three important aspects which modern day Hindu Nationalists popularly refer to as "Dharma-Dev-Desh." Dharma translates to "duty" and signifies your undying duty and loyalty towards preserving the way of life which is given by the gods. The second part is Dev, meaning "the Gods;" they are the reason why we exist and they created us and made the order established so we can develop ourselves and reach to our fullest potential. Lastly, Desh which means "country," signifies loyalty to the land in which you were born, treating it as your parents. Thoughts like this fortify a sense of ethnic nationalism in a person. To sum it up, a true folkish man or woman would be a devout ethno nationalist, cultural preserver, and believer in their ethnic gods and ancient philosophies. If you are a folkish person you are the result of countless sacrifices of your forefathers and your duty is to pass it down the line. Wear it as a badge of pride and honor, as you come from a bloodline of brave men and women who stood their ground even at sight of death. Honor your Ancestors, be proudly folkish.

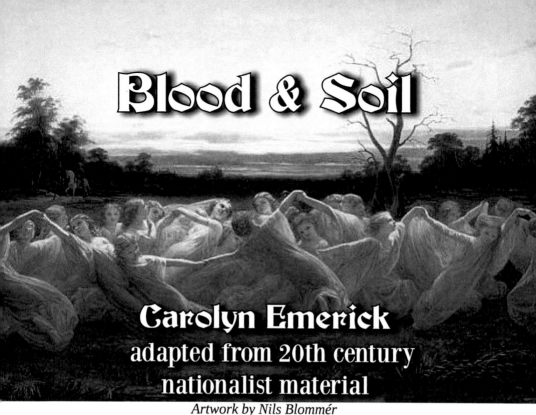

Blood & Soil

Carolyn Emerick
adapted from 20th century nationalist material

Artwork by Nils Blommér

Blood

You carry in your blood the sacred inheritance of your fathers and forefathers, of your mothers and foremothers. You do not know those blessed ancestors who have vanished in endless ranks into the darkness of the past. But they all live on in you and walk in your blood upon this earth into which their bodies have returned. Your blood is therefore something holy. In it, your parents gave you not only a physical body, but your very spirit. To deny your blood ancestry is to deny yourself. No one can change their ancestry, but we each must decide to develop the good that we have inherited and suppress the bad. To this end, we are each given the attributes of free-will and courage. It is not only a right but a duty to pass on your own blood to your children. For you are one member of the chain of generations that reaches from the past into eternity. Your place as a link means that this chain will be unbroken. Blood is the carrier of life itself. You carry in your blood the secret of creation itself. Your blood is holy, for in it live the Gods and our ancestors.

Race

Race is a combination of many factors such as genetics, physical features, skull shape, brain differences, unique language groups, continent of origin, and ancestral culture. All of these influences can cause distinct racial characteristics that make each group special and unique. Every racial group in different parts of the world have developed different characteristics that give them different attributes.

Traditionally, and demonstrable over hundreds of years, European have valued traits such as courage, loyalty, and honor as a mark of our own race. To strive for a noble mind and develop a healthy body had always been a goal to which Europeans strove. But, someone who might be quite attractive and physically fit but who possesses a soul that is not noble, that is, they live without honor, had traditionally been looked down upon in European culture.

Europe is made up of many closely related sub-races and linguistic groups. The trunk of the tree of Europa has grown from these indigenous roots. Each unique sub-group of indigenous Europeans is as special and unique as any other ethnic group in the world! And, each one contributes their own contributions to give Europe the beautiful character it possesses. Indeed, Europe is filled with its own inherent indigenous diversity, just like other continents in the world.

We, Europeans, have always had a fighting spirit. Indeed, we descend from a heroic, warrior culture! We are builders and doers. We are independent, ingenuitive, people. We are also domestic and family oriented. These traits combined to create our beautiful yet cozy cities and towns that were architecturally advanced, yet safe and comfortable - until recently. We are a people who love the arts! We created the most complex yet soulful rhapsodies of orchestral music! While, all cultures have their own folk arts and create beauty… none have mastered sculpture or painting in the way that Europa has done for centuries. Yet, while we possess this Faustian spirit of independent striving for heroism and excellence, historically, we always came together as kith, kin, clan, and tribe. The greatness of Europe, like the greatness of other cultures all around the world, stems from the soul of its own people.

The Dalai Lama understands ethnic replacement because he has seen it happen to *his* own people. In the 1990s, liberal hippies all decried the ethnic replacement of racial-Tibetans by the Han Chinese. He was right to say that Europe must remain racially European – just like Asia should remain racially Asian. North Africa and the Middle East were not racially Arab in ancient times. But these areas were colonized and settled by the Arabs, and so they remain racially Arab now. No one is challenging the Arab colonization and settlement in the lands they occupy today. The same cannot be said for ethnic Europeans – even in our indigenous homelands! When we make up only six percent of the global population!

Today, we, ethnic Europeans can find pride in our history of artists, musicians, architects, builders, explorers, thinkers, and *doers*. But, it is our ancient warrior and heroic culture that we must look to now. We must dig deep into our blood memory to find the strength, courage, and perseverance to save ourselves and the noble culture birthed by our race. For we *are* worthy and justified to assert our right to exist on this planet, just as any other race is. And, while we have birthed some of the greatest artists and builders in history, today we must dig deep into our soul to remember our ethnic *heroes*, and become heroes ourselves. We must learn to cherish the beautiful inheritance that our ancestors

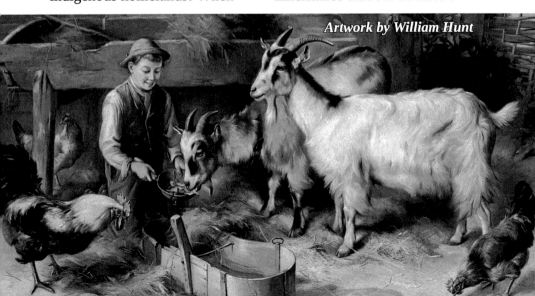

Artwork by William Hunt

have left for us, and fight to protect it for future generations.

Folk

A Folk grows from the will of the gods and the ancestors. Woe unto him who wishes to destroy the many unique and special folk cultures of the world and make all people alike. The gods created the trees, the bushes, the weeds, and the grass – not so that they could merge into one species, but that each should exist in its own special way. Just as a tree does, a Folk grows as a living whole from shared roots to become one being – the strongest of its kind; one holistic family of shared heritage. A Folk knows no state boundaries, it is bound by the ties of blood that binds all the sons and daughters of a single mother and father.

The European people is a nation of many related folk. Each ethnic-European belongs to it, no matter where he or she may live in the world. A Folk cannot be destroyed as long as its roots draw on the strength of the earth. Summer and winter may come and go, but it always blooms anew in indestructible life and perfects itself in the strength that rises from its roots towards the Gods' will. What does it mean when an individual dies? It is as if the wind blows leaves from a tree. New ones grow eternally every spring. All the different Folk groups are the greatest and most noble creation of the Gods on this earth. There is no institution in the world, no party, no *government*, and no *church*, that has the right to make them the same or rob them of even the tiniest bit of their individuality.

Homeland

O' holy heart of the Folk, the European Homeland! You were created from the endless forests and wide moors that the glaciers of the ice age left us. It was poor land only made fruitful through sweat and toil, in joy and sorrow, in endless work. One passed you on to the next and laid down in your earth from which new life grew. In you rest the endless ranks of past generations, the seed for new sowing in the wide land. The blood of the noble and brave who defended you fell on you. You were fertilized by the best that you bore.

From you, castles and cathedrals rose to the heavens, as if the earth itself wished to rise up to the god it was seeking. From our earth, from the seed of our dead, the land is broad. Under the care of industrious hands it became a garden. They protected it lovingly, like the mountains and valleys protect their villages. Proud cities by the rivers, displaying the splendor of Old Europe. The market fountain has flowed for hundreds of years here. The gates still stand through which once great kings, knights and the common folk passed.

The silver stream of fate winds through, and we find our Homeland nearly lost. The heart almost stops. How one wishes to stroke the distant forests as one would an old and beloved face. But the heart beats once more with the knowledge that we are still standing! Our castle of the knights stands as eternal testimony of European strength and virtue. There are the fields from which great eagles rose toward the sun. And there is still a memory of our heroic dead, and the eternal memorial of the continent that withstood the *world* as long as it *believed in itself*.

Everything is founded in and rests in you, our Homeland. Our strength and our greatness, but also our need and our misery. You are the ground that bore us and will bear those distant generations that will work and bleed for you. No one can live without you, but each will gladly give his life back to you who gave it to him in order to see the European Folk continue on into the future.

Artwork by Henri-Camille Danger

The Resisting Gauls: & the Yellow Vest Movement

Mariel Corriel, France

Celtic helmet found in Gaul, dated 400 BCE

In Western countries, globalization and individualism has intensified in the past decades while massive immigration has simultaneously increased. In my humble opinion, this has eroded the sense of common culture the French could have. The practice of Catholicism, common for most Frenchmen up to the mid-twentieth century, was often replaced with agnosticism and atheism later on. While only remotely linked to the ancestral creed (with the adaptation of many pagan elements), the Catholic surrogate ideology could at least serve as a means to unify the French on a common cultural ground with its weekly and yearly rituals shared by the community. Whereas I do not feel that there is a strong sense of community in today's France, we can see signs of hope surging in the usual apathy of my country.

France has been shaken by the Yellow Vests (*Gilets Jaunes* in French) picketing and demonstrating for months now. Started in reaction to the rising price of motor fuel, the economic aspect – including the constant rising taxes and the difficulty to make ends meet every month – seems to be what triggered this decentralized movement all over France. It evolved into global protests of a rare intensity, showing how much the French are fed up with the political class, its recurring failures, and the way it treats the common people. Social issues became part of the demands as the movement moved on. But who are the Yellow Vests?

Yellow Vests range across the whole political spectrum. Those living outside of urban centers appear to be the most concerned: they need their cars to commute to work and sometimes face lack of services in their areas. It is noticeable that most of these protesters are white (ethnic French). This might be due to the fact that the French countryside, small towns, and suburban areas are still mainly populated by native Frenchmen or otherwise ethnic Europeans (whose ancestors migrated during the last two centuries, assimilating for the vast majority). It leads me to make a link to the traditional (one could even say folkloric) perception the French have of

themselves. For instance it is not unusual to read on some of the demonstrators' vests and banners catchphrases mentioning the Gauls -- some proclaiming that they are "resisting Gauls," referring to an expression uttered by President Macron in Summer 2018 when he pointed out that French people are usually opposed to change.

Gauls are quite rightly perceived to be the historic ancestors of the natives of France. Romans used to associate the Gauls with roosters, a play on words on the name for a Gaul and a cock, both being called *gallus* in Latin. To this day, the rooster is still a popular emblem of France. A French saying tells that, like this bird, French people like being haughty, crowing from atop the muck-heap while actually standing in dung. This could be related to the stereotypical Frenchman who is never really satisfied about anything and likes to complain a lot. France is famous for its Revolution and its yearly strikes.

In French, *Gaul* (that is to say *gaulois*) is used as an adjective can mean bawdy, uncouth, uncultured, but also frank, upright, and free of convenance. This is a probable remnant of Gauls being perceived as barbarians or peasants, uncivilized by the Roman Empire, its Church and the Franks – later Germanic invaders who gave kings and a name to France. Note that according to etymonline.com, Gaul can be "used somewhat facetiously for a Frenchman."

To this day, Gauls are often seen as a proud people who will not be told how to behave. Whether this is grounded or just a later assumption from either state propaganda (seeing the historical united Gauls as the initial entity of what would become France) or from pop culture (as with the comic book character *Astérix* and his indomitable Gauls, whose village is the last one to resist Rome), French people seem to like this analogy. It is frequently used to describe or glorify the tenacious character of the rebel Frenchman. Thus, it is not surprising to see some Yellow Vests using that analogy.

While not reconnecting Frenchmen with their ancient roots, this protest movement shows, more than two thousand years after the Roman conquest, that the Gallic spirit may still be living on in the French. So rise up, Gauls and all peoples of the Earth! Walk on top of the filth and degeneracy filling our crumbling age, embrace your folkish heritage, and make your forebears proud! Take part in building better societies! Find in our own history and myths the strength to overcome the ordeals of today and secure your identity!

Map of Roman Gaul

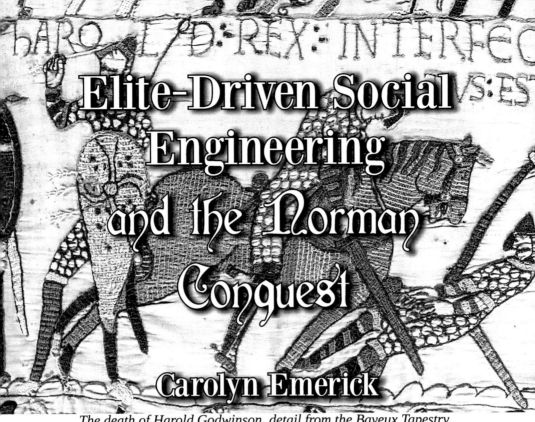

Elite-Driven Social Engineering and the Norman Conquest

Carolyn Emerick

The death of Harold Godwinson, detail from the Bayeux Tapestry

In an era when the mainstream is disparaging "old white men" with virulent hostility at every turn, I would urge society to remember our aged relatives not only with pride but with reverence. The older generations built our very nations, and they held wisdom both honed from experience as well as passed down through Western culture from the generations before them. One turn of phrase that my own grandparents said frequently is "there is nothing new under the sun." With a long-view of history, we find that there are numerous parallels and analogies to situations and issues that we face today. If we have a worldview that respects our ancestors and historical predecessors, we find that we can look to the past to glean insight and direction applicable to contemporary struggles.

Many of us would agree that we find ourselves in a great cultural struggle currently. What seems clear is that Western leadership at the highest levels has betrayed their sacred duty to protect their own nations. This betrayal does appear to be collusion between factions at the highest level of the socio-economic tier with well-connected families who consolidate power which is passed down generationally. If we look to history, we see that this is nothing new. In fact, many of these elites can trace their prestigious lines through centuries. So, in effect, there is an argument that in some cases the very same people have been in power for centuries. Therefore, examples from history of the common folk acting in resistance against elite-driven oppression and/or forced social change is very relevant to our current situation.

Indigenous Teutonic Worldview

Among the many proud ethno-cultural groups indigenous to Europe are the Teutonic peoples. Looking to early Teutonic culture, we find that this was an ethnic group quite grounded in their own tribal ethnos. Freedom and autonomy of thought and action were essential values, but rooted firmly within a cultural milieu built around the bonds of kinship. Therefore, chieftains and kings were bound to both the rule of law but also duty-bound to act as protectors of ancestral foundations of culture. A king who betrayed his tribal *ethnos* could, and would, be overthrown by the noble warrior class.

This worldview did not fit the modern dichotomy of "capitalism (individualism) versus socialism (communism)," but might be referred to as a "third position" which respected the rights of the individual with the common good of the wider tribe in mind. One example is the concept of hunting grounds held in common by the community so that any man of freeman status had the right to feed his family off the bounty of the land. However, this did not counteract the right to private land ownership. These values are important to note as they pertain to the social engineering and massive elite-driven cultural changes that the Teutonic folk would later become subjected to.

The Enslavement of the Anglo-Saxons

When the Normans conquered England, it was not simply a change of leadership regime, but a complete paradigm shift. Christianity had, of course, found its way to

England well before the Norman invasion. However, the Anglo-Saxons maintained an overtly Germanic cultural worldview which retained many of the afore mentioned values. Indeed, their Christian practice consisted of a large number of pagan belief and practice simply modified with Christian imagery. Scholar Karen Louis Jolly says, "This is Christianity succeeding by way of acculturation and Germanic culture triumphing in transformation," (Jolly, 11). This example is congruent with James C. Russell's research presented in his book, "The Germanization of Early Medieval Christianity," which discusses just how "Germanized" Christianity had to be in order to be accepted initially by the Teutonic people.

The Normans were more strictly in line with the Roman Church and brought in with them drastic changes to institutionally accepted theological perspective. Whereas, the clergy had been comparatively more in line with the worldview of the common folk in the Anglo-Saxon era, Jolly says that *"As the intellectual development of Christian doctrine increased in complexity with the advent of scholasticism in the twelfth century, the gap between the formal and the popular widened, causing some previously acceptable popular practices to appear ridiculous*

Artwork by Hans Ole Brasen

in the eyes of the new rationalists," (Jolly, 26). She is specifically speaking of religious practice, but I argue that this is a direct result and correlation with the new Norman hierarchical structure which applied to both the religious and secular spheres. What she describes is a vast chasm between the elites and the common folk, which is precisely the scenario we encounter in the Robin Hood legend. She also describes a religious parallel to the secular example of the Norman nobility scoffing at cultural customs of the Anglo-Saxons – and, of course, we know that in the High Middle Ages the line between the religious and secular spheres was virtually non-existent.

The Normans brought with them virulent economic changes. South African writer, Stephen Goodson, explained the Anglo-Saxon position on usury in his article for The Barnes Review, "The Hidden Origins of the Bank of England." He says:

"From A.D. 757 to his death in 791, the great King Offa ruled the kingdom of Mercia, one of the seven autonomous kingdoms of the Anglo-Saxon heptarchy.

Offa was a wise and able administrator and a kindhearted leader, though he could be hard on his enemies. He established the first monetary system in England (as distinguished from Romano-Keltic Britain). On account of the scarcity of gold, he used silver for coinage and as a store of wealth…. In 787 Offa introduced a statute prohibiting usury: charging of interest on money lent. The laws against usury were further entrenched by King Alfred (r. 865-99), who directed that the property of usurers be forfeited, while in 1050 Edward the Confessor (1042-66) decreed not only forfeiture, but that a usurer be declared an outlaw and be banished for life," (Goodson, 5).

Another author, David C. Douglas, discusses the close relationship between the moneylenders and the Norman monarchy in his "William the Conqueror: The Norman Impact Upon England." According to Douglas:

It is doubtful whether before the Conquest there had been any permanent Jewish settlements in England, but the existence of a Jewish community in Rouen during the central decades of the eleventh century is certain. Nor is there much doubt that a colony of these Rouen Jews came to England in the wake of the Conqueror, and was there established at his instigation... He facilitated the advent of Jews into England, and Jewry in England was throughout the twelfth century to retain not only a predominantly French character, but also special connexions with the Anglo-Norman monarchy," (Douglas, 314).

We can gain a glimpse at how this changed the lives of the peasantry in Elizabeth Caldwell Hirschman and Donald N. Yates' "The Early Jews and Muslims of England and Wales: A Genetic and Genealogical History," wherein the authors explain that William's reason for importing these moneylenders was to establish a new system of taxation whereby peasants would be forced to pay "in coin rather than in kind," (Hirshmann and Yates, 61). Under the Anglo-Saxon system, a portion of a freeman's homestead's yield could be rendered to the crown as goods. This is why in films depicting early medieval England, peasants are depicted

carrying bushels of wool, carts of livestock, etc., to their overlord. The Anglo-Saxons did, of course, use coinage, but the Normans enforced a coin-only taxation system. The relationship between the moneylending community and the Norman economic shift is further elaborated on in an article entitled "Brentry: How Norman Rule Changed England," wherein a staff writer for "The Economist" describes the changes brought in under William the Conqueror:

"Jews arrived at William's invitation, if not command, and introduced a network of credit links between his new English lands and his French ones. Unhindered by Christian usury laws, Jews were the predominant lenders in England by the 13th century. The discovery of precious metals from central European mines also helped get credit going. Jews settled in towns where there was a significant mint."

The author goes on to explain that these sweeping socio-economic changes went in tandem with the implementation of Norman domination across the landscape. Norman castles still dot the English landscape

today, standing as testament to the iron fist of Norman rule. What many today do not understand, however, is that the castle building went hand in hand with the razing of Anglo-Saxon churches. Tourists today marvel at the splendor and prestige of Norman architecture without comprehending that both castles and cathedrals are symbols of the Norman oppression of the English in mind, body, spirit, and economy. As mentioned above, Anglo-Saxons maintained a heavily Teutonic-centered cultural worldview in spite of their conversion to Christianity. In fact, these Christianized Teutons remained incredibly animistic, as is evidenced in their continued belief in wights and spirits of the land, plants, and associated with medicine. Many pagan agricultural rituals continued to be practiced with indigenous European imagery and deities swapped out for Christian ones. In many cases, the Church itself was involved with these rituals, such as the *Æcerbot* (Field Remedy) which scholar Kathleen Herbert describes in detail in her "Looking for the Lost Gods of England," (Herbert, 13-14). The Normans completely decimated the Anglo-Saxon religious presence, destroyed their churches, deposed the native English clergy which was then replaced by a Norman priesthood. This new Norman form of religion was much more heavily tied to Roman Catholic "Christendom." The staff author at The Economist explains, "To fund the infrastructure heavier taxes had to be levied on peasants, which 'forced them to work harder.'"

Of course, the Anglo-Saxons did not surrender willingly or easily. The Battle of Hastings in 1066 was only the first of many devastating blows. Today in the right wing, there is a lot of discussion of more recent Bolshevik orchestrated atrocities such as Holodomor, the man-made famine that killed millions of Ukrainians under the Soviet regime, and the horrors of Stalin's work camps. But, the strong parallels between the havoc wrought by communism and the economic enslavement of the English and genocidal behaviors of the Normans is ignored. Not only did the Normans usher in a new religious ideology that was enforced by rule of law as a tool to control the populace, but

what might be called Holodomor 1.0 was unleashed against the good people of Northern England in what would be remembered as "The Harrying of the North." James Aitcheson, writing for History Today, says:

"The Harrying, which took place over the winter of 1069–70, saw William's knights lay waste to Yorkshire and neighbouring shires. Entire villages were razed and their inhabitants killed, livestock slaughtered and stores of food destroyed. This scorched-earth operation is one of the defining episodes of the Conquest, not just from a military-political perspective but also in terms of how it has shaped modern perceptions of the Normans as a tyrannical and merciless warrior class.

The object of the campaign was two-fold. First, William sought to flush out and eliminate the Northumbrian rebels. More importantly, by destroying the region's resources so comprehensively, he sought to put an end to the cycle of rebellions by ensuring that any future insurgents would lack the means to support themselves. The campaign was as efficient as it was effective. William's armies spread out over more than one hundred miles of territory, as far north as the River Tyne. The 12th-century chronicler John of Worcester writes that food was so scarce in the aftermath that people were reduced to eating not just horses, dogs and cats but also human flesh."

We can see quite plainly that the Normans unleashed a campaign of terror against the good folk of England while also completely changing their economy and utilizing religious ideology as a means of enforcement. The similarities to both the Soviet regime and elite-driven social engineering today are striking. For an ethno-culture to whom freedom and individual autonomy were as valued as the bonds of kinship, and who valued their cultural heritage and identity to the degree that heroic tales of valor from their origins in pagan Scandinavia continued to be told in the mead halls, this enslavement would have been insufferable. In addition to a new form of religion, confiscation of personal property, a new and foreign economic system, and the massive loss of life, the Normans also took away the beloved Teutonic communal woodlands.

A Legendary Folk Hero Arises

It is within this context that the legendary tales of Robin Hood would arise. While the Robin Hood figure with which we are familiar is legendary, most scholars are in agreement that the heroic figure was likely born from a historical person or is an amalgam of several figures who were known and remembered in folklore due to their resistance to Norman subjugation. This places the tale

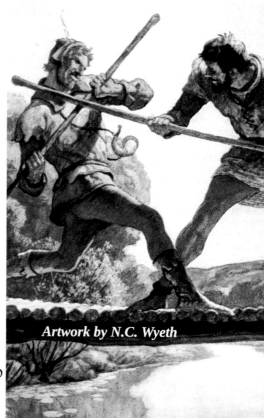

Artwork by N.C. Wyeth

in the realm of mytho-history, as it discusses the life and escapades of figures who are impossible to verify; however, it is set squarely in a historical time and place and the themes rife within are perfectly in line with the concerns of the era. But separating what is fact from what is fiction is secondary from the lessons that the tales have to offer us as we navigate our way through our current society ruled by oppressive elites who seem hell bent on suppressing the white man while they socially engineer our nations through means of ideological psychological warfare and massive demographic replacement.

When we look to the character of Robin Hood, we see an archetypal woodsman who lives by an ancient primal code of honor. Rather than confronting the ruling class on their turf, he chooses to step outside of their matrix all together. He removes himself from economic dependence on the ruling class by living independently off the land, doubling down on the Teutonic ethnic traditional way of life. But, he is not a lone-wolf, as it were. His "band of merry men"

show us that while many of us today feel alone, we are not. There are others who see the tyranny, the social engineering, and who oppose it. Therefore we can also step outside of their matrix and create our own communities based on shared values. We, too, can take from the rich to feed the poor by way of choosing how we spend our own coin. If we begin to see our brethren as "folk" once again, we can turn our eyes upon our own community building. In Teutonic culture, bonds of kinship and tribe were considered something sacred. Therefore, conscious intention to spend our coin in ways that support of our folk who stand in solidarity against those who would see us destroyed can be considered a "folk tithe."

But, Robin Hood's primary function as an archetype of resistance to tyranny presents a message that is both basic and crucial. *We must resist.* We must resist at all costs the dark future that the social engineers are attempting to funnel us toward. Robin Hood, therefore, is a figure who embodies hope. His gang of unlikely brothers are not called the angry men, the depressive men, the hopeless men. No, they are the *merry men*. And why should they be happy living under the oppressive, murderous regime described above? Robin Hood and his merry men remind us that we have everything to live for. We are not dead yet. We are still standing. We have a glorious heritage and a beautiful culture. Again, looking to my own ancestors with the honor and reverence that they deserve, I remember when I had difficult times in my youth, my English-heritage grandmother always told me, "you come from strong stock." And I would say to you: *We* come from strong stock. And we *will* endure.

Bibliography:

Aitcheson, James. The Harrying of the North. 12 October 2016. <https://www.historytoday.com/james-aitcheson/harrying-north>.

Douglas, David C. William the Conqueror: The Norman Impact Upon England. University of California Press, 1967. Print.

Goodson, Stephen. "The Hidden Origins of the Bank of England." The Barnes Review XVIII.5 (2012): 5-14.

Herbert, Kathleen. Looking for the Lost Gods of England. Anglo-Saxon Books, 1994. Print.

Hirschman, Elizabeth Caldwell and Donald N. Yates. The Early Jews and Muslims of England and Wales: A Genetic and Genealogical History. McFarland, 2014.

Jolly, Karen Louis. Popular Religion in Late Saxon England. Chapel Hill: The University of North Carolina Press, 1996. Print.

Owen, Francis. The Germanic People: Their Origin and Expansion. Dorset Press, 1960. Print.

Russel, James C. The Germanization of Early Medieval Christianity. Oxford: Oxford University Press, 1994. Print.

Staff writer. "Brentry: How Norman Rule Shaped England." December 2016. The Economist. Web.

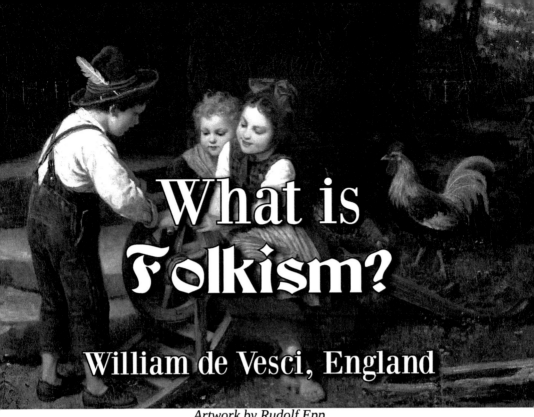

What is Folkism?

William de Vesci, England

Artwork by Rudolf Epp

In the period after the twilight of absolute monarchy, numerous ideologies began to spring up across Europe as ordinary people found themselves able to give expression to their political desires for the first time in our history. Political power was no longer restricted to those of the upper classes, who saw the world in terms of fiscal liberalism or parliamentarianism, for instance. The latter of these random examples became a given for the peoples of Europe, thus enabling them to experiment with whatever

ideology the human mind, fueled by the collective unconscious, could possibly imagine. This gave rise to a long list of political creeds; socialism, communism, revolutionary conservatism, social democracy and so on, all of which have been tried and tested in some way, shape or form, since universal franchise. The more prominent of these – socialism, communism, fascism, to name but a few – we are well acquainted with. Some, however, we understand considerably less. The focus of the article, Folkism, is an ideology that exists in and of itself, as well as serving as a foundational ideology built on by other ideologies tried and tested in the form of governmental power. Considering its broad reach throughout modern history, it's surprising that so few people have a credible understanding of Folkism.

Origins of Folkism

Folkism emerged as a quasi-mainstream movement in 19th century Germany as a belated response to centuries of disunity and imperial rule by autocratic Christian monarchs. Heavily linked to National Romanticism, *die Völkische Bewegung* (Folkish Movement) drew much of its early inspiration from philosophers of German Idealism, most notably Johann Gottlieb Fichte (*Addresses to the German Nation*, 1808), but also from others such as Georg Wilhelm Friedrich Hegel and, to a lesser extent, Arthur Schopenhauer. Paradoxically, given his critiques of German Idealism, the German Folkish movement later adopted certain Nietzschean tendencies, too. The crucial tenets of this early Völkism consisted of an ethnic nationalism fueled by mystical/spiritual attachment to The Fatherland, along with a growing suspicion of industrialization and the alienation and atomization within society that it stimulated.

Ties to Romanticism

As it can be discerned from this link to mysticism and spirituality, the early Folkish movement was closely intertwined with Romanticism which, in Germany at that time, heavily focused on folklore and an anti-urban, back to the land ideology. It can be said, without accusations of an overreach, that brothers Jakob and Wilhelm Grimm provided much inspiration for the early Völkisch adherents, as did legendary composer Richard Wagner. As the movement progressed into the 20th century, and as Germany lay disarmed and dishonored in the wake of World War I, it began to adopt an even deeper spiritual element that incorporated Pagan revivalism, as practiced by the folkish Thule Society (est. 1918), and heavily focusing on Germanic Pagan texts such as the Prose and Poetic Eddas. This accentuated the spiritual aspect of Folkism, whilst also providing it with a particularism and esoteric character to the outside observer, which it has become closely associated with – one of its few associations to have survived into the modern era. The post-war atmosphere also reinvigorated the movement's strive for self-determination pertaining to all members of the nation, despite their falling outside of the arbitrarily defined national borders of the era. It's interesting to note that at this time, Folkism wasn't exclusive to the political right; socialists also adopted their phraseology, using it to romanticize the proletariat whilst avoiding the racial undertones adopted by nationalist circles.

It's worth mentioning another, non-German folkish movement (of sorts), namely that of the "Merrie Olde England" romanticists of the 19th century. In modern times, this sentiment has been derided and its propagators dubbed "little Englanders", a slur which the imperialists once used to christen the liberal romanticists who sought a cultural revival within the borders of England at the turn of the 20th century. However, despite this negative connotation, the movement remains valid. It was best exemplified by the verse of poets such as William Blake, A.E. Houseman and, perhaps, Rudyard Kipling (select poems). The romanticist movement even found expression in the literature of legendary fiction writer Thomas Hardy (a recommended author for anybody with an interest in Folkish politics). Hardy wrote extensively about a quasi-fictional world that's become known colloquially as "Hardy's Wessex" – as the name suggests, this setting covered much of the ancient Anglo-Saxon Kingdom of

Artwork by Rudolf Epp

Wessex, and was romanticised to include extensive Folkish elements. This movement was also associated with pre-Marxist English socialism, as expressed by artists such as Walter Crane, who designed a May Day poster appealing to Folkish and socialist sentiment in the late 19th century.

Folkism and Politics

Sadly, an historical account of the Folkish movement, however brief, cannot avoid curtly examining its association with and influence on (or lack thereof) National Socialism. It's plainly evident that the NSDAP adopted Völkisch phraseology and iconography from its early days; the symbolism used by the party and its elite paramilitary wing, the SS (Schutzstafffel), emanated from the same source as that of Folkism, whilst "The German Folk" (das Deutsche Volk) became a staple of the Nazi lexicon. Leading National Socialist ministers and members counted among the higher circles of Völkisch thought included Heinrich Himmler (Reichsführer SS), Walther Darré (Agriculture) and Alfred Rosenberg (Eastern Territories), as well as Hans Günther (Universities Jena, Berlin and Freiburg). Given his association and close collaboration with National Socialism, one might also be inclined to include Martin Heidegger in this list, especially given his critique of urban living so familiar amongst Folkish circles, although this might be something of a stretch. Völkisch thought found expression in the iconography of the SS, the agrarian tendencies of Nazism under Darré and essays appearing in the Völkischer Beobachter which was, in the beginning, under the editorship of Rosenberg. However, these tendencies were counterbalanced by leading functionaries in the Führer's inner circle, including Adolf Hitler himself, who had no time for romanticism. In private conversations amongst his inner circle, Hitler derided some of his colleagues for their overly romanticist tendencies and openly mocked the idea of "Wotan worship," evidently an allusion to Himmler's preoccupation with Germanic Paganism and the occult. It also became clear that, with the advent of WWII, Germany's state mechanisms had firmly reverted to Prussian militarism ahead of any notion of Folkish sentiment or romanticism.

And thus, as the guns fell silent in April 1945, Folkish ideology lay in ruins along with the rest of Germany and Europe. Tainted by the horrors of WWII, it has yet to make a reappearance in national political life anywhere in Western Europe, with those who have dared to espouse it accused of everything from racialism and violence to antisemitism and genocidal intent. This is a fairly lazy derision typical of a society "blessed" with a stubborn, obstinate even, contempt for ideology of any kind. Today, the "i" word is synonymous with everything negative that occurred in the 20th century, with ideology being considered cognate with the utopian and, consequently, unattainable and irrational to pursue. Yet this fails to analyze the benefits, or lack thereof, of any given ideology, including Folkism, objectively. It presupposes that it's bad purely on account of it being an ideology. This is a grave shame, for it has much to offer the modern world and could, perhaps, provide an antidote for some of the more toxic aspects of modernity. For that reason, we must now pick apart Folkism, establish what it stands for relevant to the various spheres of social, political and economic life today, whilst refusing to discredit it by association with alleged historical culpability.

True Folkism

The biggest clue as to what this ideological persuasion stands for is in the name; Folk. Unlike abstract ideologies such as capitalism and Marxism, which view the world solely through the lens of materialism, Folkism's primary concern is with the folk; the people. Capitalism and Marxism both take the view that social wellbeing is downstream from material wealth, thus they assume the former will take care of itself provided they (the capitalists or Marxists) ensure the economy manifests in a way conducive to this end. This was very much the view taken by American sociologists in the post-war era, who posited that National Socialism spread throughout Germany in response to the severe economic misfortunes of the 1920s. Equally and, somewhat paradoxically given their materialist commonalities, they also believed that in order to stave off communism in Western Europe, material concerns must never be permitted to escalate beyond "ordinary" levels. Whilst this latter point translated into policy that achieved the stated aim, either through cause and effect or sheer coincidence, it was born out of an extremely simplistic view of human nature. To assume that humanity's concerns lay primarily in the material world is simply false. This has manifested in a modern society that, despite possessing material wealth like none other in history, is severely lacking in mental wellbeing as a result of ethno-cultural and spiritual decimation, with the result being that almost a quarter of Europeans consume prescription anti-depressants as a matter of course and all measures of an unhealthy society – divorce, deviancy, violent crime and so on – are showing massive increases. Folkism rightly rejects this simplistic, materialistic view of social wellbeing and instead provides a more holistic solution to society's ills.

Social solidarity is a key tenet of Folkism. Under a capitalist system, social solidarity is non-existent, whilst Marxist tendencies promulgate a pseudo-solidarity which simply sets one socio-economic class of

Artwork by Richard Ansdell

a nation against another. Neither of these options are suitable in a Folkish society. Folkism seeks to build social solidarity based on membership of a nation, in its truest sense; membership of the national community, and solidarity therein, derives from the original meaning of the word *nation*, that is a people who share a common language, culture, heritage and ethnicity. Regardless of socio-economic status, a fellow national comrade should be shown the solidarity that workers allegedly show one another in a Marxist society. This brings down the divisive dichotomy of working-class vs ownership-class, instead creating a classless society in which the lowliest peasant is valued as a national comrade, just as a member of the aristocracy would be, or a "middle-class" small business owner. Unlike a Marxist society, Folkish social solidarity places greater emphasis on shared culture, as opposed to material wealth. The culture of a nation should be shared by all its members and those of various socio-economic status should have no qualms with partaking in cultural activities with those poorer or richer than himself.

This is a vast departure from what we know today, where social classes are encouraged to show animosity towards one another and operate within entirely different and separate cultural spheres. This is a poisonous trap engineered deliberately by those materialists who seek to rule by the principles of divide and conquer and must be totally rejected.

The Capitalist Question

For similar reasons, Folkism must inherently reject capitalism as an economic philosophy. Houston Stewart Chamberlain wrote in 1915 that "capitalism has turned the English into an urban nation dominated by a vulgar, money-grubbing, philistine middle-class incapable of any sort of culture", and his assessment was absolutely correct and equally applicable to any Western society today. Folkism seeks to destroy the worship of the false idols of materialism, asserting that true happiness and national comradeship is to be found in pursuits that transcend mere economics and instead permeate all aspects of national life, whether they be cultural, social or even spiritual. Capitalism breeds an unhealthy one-upmanship attitude that merely serves the divide and rule agenda of a *faceless elite,* an elite which derives its power from national comrades fighting against one another for material gain, instead of side-by-side for material and cultural comfort.

To replace this capitalist poison, an entirely new philosophy of Folkish Socialism is proposed. Folkish Socialism fuses the aforementioned ideology of classless national comradeship with economic principles that ensure no member of the folk is left behind or denied their opportunity to contribute towards the collective – and therefore personal – material wellbeing of the nation. It also rejects this Western trend of placing life's sustenance in the hands of greedy, unaccountable, profit-driven capitalists who care not for the folk, only for their own pockets. To this end, Folkish Socialism asserts that only the collective folk has the right to own the raw materials necessary to sustain life. Furthermore, Folkish Socialism rejects any economic enterprise which could damage the folk.

Personal development and progression is greatly encouraged, provided it's not pursued at the expense of one's national comrades. For this reason, generic capitalist chains that spring up in every High St. are treated like enemy tanks; in their place, local small enterprise is encouraged to become the centre of a community's economic life, replacing the soulless franchise operations that have ensured 21st century town centres resemble every other town centre anywhere in the world. Not only does this detract from the culture of a locality, it also harms individuals who aren't able to penetrate the local market as a result of these multinational market-saturating monstrosities.

Nature & the Environment

Another core socio-economic principle of Folkism is agrarianism. European peoples are ill-adjusted to urban life; their nature is inclined to the land and, therefore, this is the setting of their most productive and creative endeavors. Why must we force Europeans, like cattle, into cities in the name of imaginary "progress?" This hyper-urbanized society in which we live serves no purpose other than to line the pockets of shareholders of multinational corporations, many of which produce nothing and contribute nothing to human advancement. In any event, living conditions within urban environments are drastically worse than in a rural setting; population density is high, increasing the spread of disease; pollution shaves years off one's life expectancy through atmospheric carcinogens; fresh air, thus, is of a minimum, and 24/7 living vastly decreases mental wellbeing. We should promote and strive for, within the Folkish movement, a large-scale *return to the land*, which entails society relying on the fruits of its own labor – which is infinitely more rewarding – as opposed to cheap foreign imports of undesirable quality. Through agrarian policies, Northern European peoples can be freed from toxic urban living and instead return to a more harmonious existence intrinsic to their natural habitat; the land. After all, Folkism subscribes wholeheartedly that a people is comprised of and shaped by the two fundamental, eternal partners that have existed

Artwork by Hans Ole Brasen

complementary to one another for thousands of years; *blood and soil*. No more can a people be separated from its soil than it can from its blood.

This engenders living in a way which complements another key facet of Folkish ideology, namely that of environmentalism. The modern left often airs its alleged moral righteousness on this issue, taking aim at capitalism for its flagrant attacks on our environment. Whilst their assessment of the cause is at least partially valid, their solutions to tackle this dilemma are woefully inadequate. For one cannot pledge to build millions of houses annually for environmentally antagonistic aliens to the national community and preserve green spaces and natural habitats simultaneously.

Animals & The Land

Equally, a multiracial society comprised of peoples with vastly different concepts of animal welfare cannot coexist with the desire to improve the lives of the animals which capitalism horrendously exploits. Folkism proposes new, modern solutions to these problems. At the center of these is the rejection of capitalist exploitation of animal life, which places the desire for quick profit miles ahead of compassion and the duty of care we Northern Europeans have towards animals. Furthermore, Folkism rejects the importation of those alien to the national community whose nature it is not to care for animals. Folkism maintains that its fundamental to the Northern European soul to be wedded with an innate desire to assuage any suffering one sees in beings within our remit of care. This does not necessarily demonstrate a preference towards veganism, for the food chain and laws of nature are to be respected.

However, this does mean placing the rights of animals above the right man currently claims to abuse said animals. This means, in practice, that immoral, profit-driven practices such as live exports and factory farming must be viewed most unfavorably, whilst a zero tolerance policy towards animal cruelty must be adhered to. Those who believe it is their right to cause unnecessary suffering to animals must be excluded from the national community, by force if necessary.

Whilst the topic of environmentalism has been, for the most part, covered in the preceding chapter briefly outlining Folkism's agrarian philosophy, it merits slightly more exploration. Folkism rejects progress, or perceived progress, which endangers the future of our planet. For this reason, it rejects unsustainable sources of energy, favoring renewable or environmentally friendly alternatives. Folkism also rejects the concretization of our land, seeking not just to cease further building projects, but to actively demolish and re-naturalize much of what presently exists in concrete form.

Ethnic Faith

A potentially more tricky subject to address and define is that of spirituality. As it has been made clear by inference and association, Folkish ideology is largely incompatible with the capitalistic ambitions of mass Protestantism and the unearthly aspirations of Catholic Christianity. It is also plainly evident that the ethnocentrism of Folkish ideology places it in antipathy to Christian teachings of proselytizing the barbarian. However, these are mere surface clashes that allude to a deeper problem; Christianity has failed Northern Europeans, something quite obvious from the rate at which the religion is collapsing in this region and has been for a hundred years. In the wider context of history, Christianity has existed in these lands for an incredibly small amount of time before its inevitable demise. Indo-European peoples trace their roots back to many millennia before the Common Era, and Christianity has been the dominant religious force in Northern Europe for less than a single millennium, in some regions. It can also be said that Northern Europe has only ever been nominally Christian; the old Pagan rites and rituals have survived and been absorbed by Christian teaching to the point that the latter's festivals don't represent the Orthodoxy in any way. One thinks of Christmas, characterized by Yule Trees, Yule Logs, a great feast and so on, whilst Easter's (Christianized version of Ostara) symbolism is almost exclusively pre-Christian – the eggs, the hare, chicks and children's games all being symbols of fertility in the archaic Northern European tradition. Thus reverting to our ancient ways, with a more nuanced understanding of the divine than Christianity can provide us with, is no more unnatural than resuming the use of one's native tongue after returning from a trip abroad. This also means that Folkism seeks to revive a native spirituality that has lived on within the *collective unconscious* (soul) of Northern Europeans, suffering suppression but never extinction – one cannot extinct artificially what exists primordially. This allows Northern Europeans to embrace their nature, as opposed to repressing it artificially, which in turn will contribute to an enhanced psychological wellbeing and spiritual harmony this part of the world has sorely missed over the last thousand years. Finally, native Northern European spirituality possesses the key advantage of being an *ethnic faith,* which enables it to complement the other key facets of Folkism.

Folkism vs. Globalism

Before we conclude this historical and ideological summary of Folkish Ideology, there are a few issues to be settled. Obviously, from the other philosophical points, one can patently ascertain that Folkism stands diametrically opposed to globalism and socio-economic globalization. One cannot stand for ethnic solidarity with one's national comrades and simultaneously adopt the Marxist doctrine of "workers of the world unite" – they're simply incompatible. Nor can the capitalist dictate which stipulates economic unity throughout the world, under the leadership of a certain hyper-power of course, be in any way reconciled with the Folkish *Weltanschauung.* For this reason – and this remains a sensitive topic of discussion –

Folkish ideology stands opposed to the proponents of globalism, represented by a very specific group coordinating this message from both the left and the right. Their interests and ours can never be reconciled. In a somewhat related point of discussion and, for similar reasons, Folkism rejects bourgeois culture and world-view as a matter of course. Whilst this may seemingly contradict with the desire to institute a classless national community, Folkism views bourgeois culture as one of the fundamental obstacles to achieving this. For bourgeois culture is inherently international and elitist, rendering it simply incompatible with Folkish ideas of social solidarity and a cultural environment shared by all members of the national community. And finally – and briefly, in the interest of avoiding repetition – we must make a crucial distinction of terminology; many politicians today seek to appeal to "the masses," this faceless, malleable and interchangeable group who simply happen to occupy a nation's borders at any given time, a group archaically referred to as *"laios."* Folkish ideology seeks to replace this identification with the *ethnos* which, as can be inferred, refers to the folk, a national community that is bound by blood, fixed and impermeable. It's worth stressing this point, for it's easily misunderstood.

To conclude: Folkish Ideology is both historical, being firmly rooted in the 19th century, and modernist, adopting radical solutions to the problems of tomorrow. This differentiates it from the plurality of political ideologies that exist in the Western world today. It's also the only ideology that combines a coherent world-view encompassing all aspects of existence, not merely economic platforms as is the trend with the other parties and cliques. It promotes economic wellbeing, but also recognizes the paramount importance and vitality of spiritual and social wellbeing which cannot be found anywhere else across the ideological spectrum. It holds the keys to Northern Europe's survival as a distinct society and is the only implementable doctrine that can avert the disaster that has become almost inevitable. We must begin to see the value in Folkish ideology once more, for our very existence depends on it. No more can we sit comfortably within the myopic paradigm of liberal and conservative, endemic of our epoch. Only by returning to the timeless, primordial doctrine of Folkish Ideology may we rid ourselves of the shackles that have all but defeated us over the last thousand years.

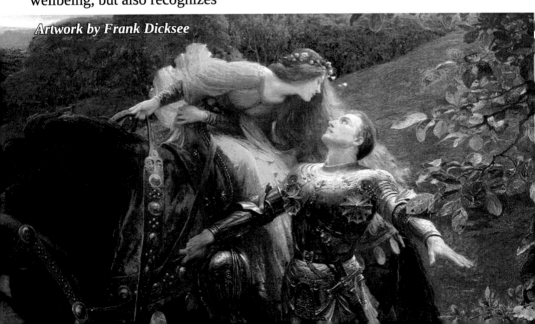

Artwork by Frank Dicksee

Racial Faith

Saxo Rikardson, USA

Artwork by William Bouguereau

Race and Faith are not two separate things.

There is a pandemic of a notion that Race and Faith are two separate things; this notion that any Faith can belong to any Race, and that any Race can hold any Faith. For example, a person of European descent can be a Christian or a Hindu, etc. Likewise, a Hindu need not be an Indian, and a Christian can be white or black, etc. In this notion, Race and Faith are independent of each other and either can be little more than an adjective to be tacked onto the other. This misbegotten notion is not held by any one group of people. No single ideology, political party, race, country, social class, or any entity is solely guilty of holding this notion. In fact, it would be easier to list those who do not hold a world-view tainted by this notion than those who do. And this is exactly why I feel the need to write this article to point out a truth that has been lost on many people.

First, I must clarify specifically why this notion has negative ramifications for humanity at large so that the importance of this topic is understood. This notion of separable Race and Faith is not entirely a completely modern idea, although modernity has indeed frequently used this notion to separate people from their folk-identity. But, the roots of this notion started much sooner than that. Although much of the blame can indeed be put on the Abrahamists, especially the early Christian and Muslim zealot armies who wielded their weaponized religious ideology more like a political tool than an actual religion, it is not entirely their fault either. Zoroastrianism and Buddhism are two other "revealed" universalist religions which shoulder some of the burden of guilt. To be clear, the blame rests on all of these religions, not any single one of them in particular.

So, why did these universalist religions come about in the first place? As mentioned above, the Abrahamic religions of Christianity and Islam were founded or popularized in regions where a group was seeking to expand and solidify their power as an empire. Constantine and the Roman elite legitimized Christianity to end the numerous cults of Rome and unify Faith as a political tool to control their multi-ethnic populace, Mohamed founded Islam to unite the Arabs in a global domination directive and subjugate conquered people to serve them, the Persians did likewise with Zoroastrianism, and Gautama Buddha originated in the Indian subcontinent - a place with many warring kingdoms and several religions. All these origins have one thing in common: a governing faction ruling many diverse ethnic groups within their territory, and the desire to unite their subjects and solidify their power over them. The ugly and sickening truth is these religions were not created or popularized as actual Faith. They were political tools created by rulers to keep their human thralls in their pens.

It should also be noted that the people these rulers controlled were not faithless. They all - each and every single one - possessed a unique Faith to their Race. Sure, they all had similarities: a pantheon of gods, ancestor worship, animism, all could be described as shared traits. But, the gods in the pantheon, the ancestors being worshiped, and even the nature of the animism were unique to that specific folk. But, then, these psychopathic rulers, not caring about the sacredness of these Faiths to these Races, stripped them of their unique ethnic Faiths thereby shattering their identities. They were given new identities as subjects of the ruling class. For example, you were no longer a proud Anglo-Saxon worshiping Woden and his tribe of gods, nor your proud ancestors who came and conquered the British Isles, but instead a feudal serf paying your dues to the Catholic Church and serving your king, appointed by a foreign God. And, of course, your folk weren't the only ones who experienced such a fate. You shared this shameful life of subjugation with the Iberians in Spain, the Hungarians, and many others the world wide, all to cement the power of your rulers, be they secular or religious.

It should come as no surprise that all four religions are still around; and two of them, Christianity and Islam, are still expanding their global reach. Why would they not, when the rulers who used these religions, concerned so much with their earthly power, did so much to make this so? And therein lies the fundamental problem with all of these religions, but especially Christianity, Islam, Buddhism: this very notion of separable Faiths and Races. All of it descended from, and arguably still is nothing more than, a political tool to enslave you and your ancestors.

This is also why Folkright is right for folk all across the world. To return to an earlier example: you cannot truly call yourself a "proud Anglo-Saxon" while you are still enslaved by a politicized religious ideology that puts your allegiance to an entity other than your own people. Your identity is still broken for as long as your allegiance is divided. Only by returning to hailing your own ethnic gods and worshiping your own blood ancestors can you truly be that "proud Anglo-Saxon" (or any other ethnic identity) you claim to be. This is because Faith is a vital component to your Race, intrinsic to its identity, not merely an adjective to tack onto it. And that is where Folkright asserts a path. We seek to end these political tools and encourage all Races to repair themselves by reviving their own unique Faiths from the brink of death.

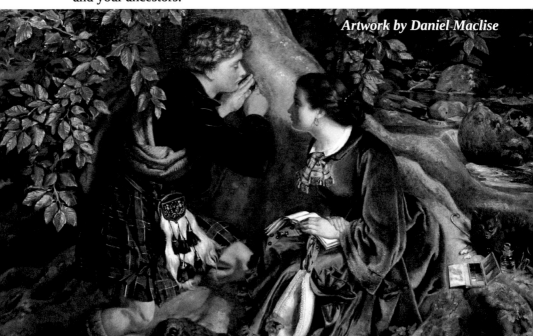

Artwork by Daniel Maclise

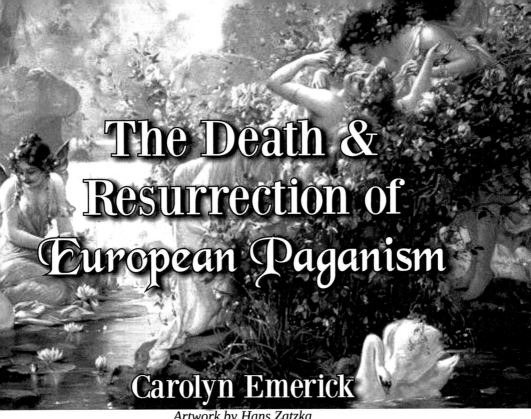

The Death & Resurrection of European Paganism

Carolyn Emerick

Artwork by Hans Zatzka

Modern Confusion

Shamanism, spiritualism, energy work, rainbows and crystals, totems and spirit animals. In our modern world, these things have existed in the realm of either "exotic" (non-white) cultures or have been snugly in the possession of lefty wingnuts. In the sphere of Western paganism, there has been a great deal of discussion about reconnecting to holistic living which is often connected to "we are all one" ideology. The irony is that Europeans did, in fact, hold an animistic understanding of the world at one point in time. We, too, believed in an interconnectedness of life and fluidity between the spirit and mundane realms. In fact, the mortal world was not actually mundane at all. It was teeming with spiritual life-force to the degree that you might say that Midgard, the land of mortals in the Teutonic worldview, was seen as *enchanted*.

It is fair to say that Europeans viewed the earth and life itself in a way not dissimilar to various indigenous spiritual traditions in the world. Indeed, animistic polytheism rooted in ancestor veneration was virtually a universal faith for humanity. However, it was not *universalist*. Spirituality was a unique expression tailored to each ethnic-group. So, while many themes can be found throughout the world in various ethnic faiths, each ethnic faith also varies with particulars and peculiarities that are specific to the people practicing it. In recent years, the revival of animism and belief in the metaphysical that sees human beings as interconnected with each other and our environment has tended to go hand in hand with the liberal doctrine that all human beings are one. But this is anachronistic. While the various peoples of the past, that is prior to Abrahamic universalism, did hold many of the same or similar spiritual beliefs, they were cognizant of the reality of race and other ethnic differences.

In other words, two different tribal groups may well have seen the landscape teeming with spirits, viewed themselves as interacting with both the spiritual and material, and very likely believed in notions such as a cosmic web that connects all things. However, this in no way influenced people not to draw boundaries, borders, and engage in self-defense against neighboring rivals. In fact, it was universalist Christianity, not paganism, that was often used to make people forget their differences and join together in one ideological club. There was a clear understanding that the "one God" ideology was correlated with "one people" under "one king." This is why Christianity was adopted by pagan kings looking to consolidate their power and expand their territory. Mono-theism was useful to the feudal notion of monarchy. Mono-theism was a tool to create mono-culture which helped to erase the differences between conquered tribes as they were merged into larger kingdoms. Therefore, the notion that an animistic worldview is equated with modern liberal "one world" nonsense is anachronistic to historical pagan practice.

European Worldview versus Abrahamism

An article by an author using the pen-name "Spengler" on the Christian web-journal called "First Things" sheds some light on this. The article,

"Christian, Muslim, Jew," highlights the writings of a Jewish rabbi called Franz Rosenzweig. While Rosenzweig died in 1929, the author says that his philosophy was especially popular in the post-WWII era. Spengler describes World War II as a war between Abrahamism and "neopaganism," saying that "after neopaganism nearly conquered Europe, Rosenzweig's contention that Christianity requires the presence of the Jews found great resonance." He continues:

> "*Pagans, Rosenzweig explained, have only the fragile and ultimately futile effort to preserve their physical continuity through blood and soil. Their hope for immortality takes the form of a perpetual fight for physical existence, which one day they must lose. Rosenzweig's sociology of religion thus offers unique insights into the origin and nature of civilizational conflict when he argues that a pagan people, ever sentient of the fragility of their existence, are always prepared to fight to the death.*"

Much has been said over the years about paganism continuing to live on in the hearts and minds of ethnic Europeans. Rosenzweig's view is that the presence of Jews in the West is a sort of paternalistic role which stops Europeans from reverting to paganism, with Gnostic Christianity being a form of Christianity that merges indigenous spiritual worldview with Abrahamic scripture. Spengler says that Rosenzweig *"began a new kind of dialogue between Judaism and Christianity when he argued that the two faiths complement each other: Christianity to propagate revelation to the world, and Judaism to 'convert the inner pagan' inside each Christian."* He later continues, "Rosenzweig's most influential claim holds that the Jew 'converts the inner pagan' inside the Christian, such that the living presence of the Jewish people creates a counterweight to the Gnostic impulses in Christianity."

Rosenzweig's worldview clearly saw Judaism and Christianity working together in unity against a "blood and soil" worldview. Paganism is essentially ancestor worship and nature veneration, literally blood and soil. And, according to Rosenzweig, without the guiding hand of Judaism, Europeans would fall back into this belief system. Spengler explains, "Rosenzweig argues that pagan society cannot foster authentic human individuality but dissolves the individual into an extension of race or state." This explains quite well how closely paganism is tied to ethnicity, whereas Christianity, guided by Judaism, is supposed to function as a universalizing force transcending racial boundaries. He continues on:

"In pagan society, where God remains unrevealed, the individual exists only as an organ of the collective of state or race. The pagan's sense of immortality therefore depends solely on the perpetuation of his race, and his most sacred act is to sacrifice himself in war to postpone the inevitable day when his race will go down in defeat."

I would say that this Jewish rabbi's views on paganism are accurate. And his discussion illuminates precisely why Christianity was used as the ideological tool to subdue disparate tribes into submission under an expanding empire with globalist aims. Indeed, if you begin to dig through old dictionaries for the definition of the word "ethnic," what one finds is that before WWII, it had been used interchangeably with "heathen" and "pagan." The word *"ethnos"* itself has origins in ancient Greek wherein it was used to describe a collective group of creatures that are alike

Artwork by Mihael Stroj

to one another. In the earliest usage, *ethnos* could be used interchangeably with words like hive, pack, flock, etc. However, it was also used to describe groups of people who were alike, such as a tribe or a race. The New Testament verse Romans 10:2 supports Rabbi Rosenzweig's point of view: "For there is no difference between the Jew and the Greek: for the same Lord over all is rich unto all that call upon him." Add to this that the word used by Saul-turned-Paul of Tarsus in the original Greek New Testament which has been translated into English as "pagan" was originally "*ethnikos.*" It is quite clear that Rosenzweig was correct. Christianity had a directive to remove barriers between ethnicity while paganism was synonymous with ethnic identity. Therefore, liberal hippy-dippy pagans pushing no borders are practicing the wrong religion!

Conspicuous Origins of Wicca

But, how did this confused form of paganism begin? In light of what "Spengler" said about Rosenzweig's views of paganism and Spengler's own assertion that World War II was "neopaganism nearly conquering Europe," it is interesting to look at the birth of Wicca. Modern liberal pagans owe a debt of gratitude to Gerald Gardner, the founder of Wicca. It is important to note that pagan revivalist movements have popped up in virtually every century in Western history. The notion that modern pagan practice originated with the advent of Wicca is false. Further, Wicca is not a reconstructed pagan faith, but rather a contrived religion cobbled together with bits and pieces from Germanic and Celtic belief mixed together with ceremonial magic. According to his Wikipedia biography, Gardner was a freemason.

It is curious that Gardner appeared on the scene the same year that World War II came to a close. Gardner's Wikipedia article explains: "moving to London in 1945, he became intent on propagating this religion, attracting media attention." Witchcraft had been outlawed in Britain for centuries, but the Witchcraft Act was repealed under Winston Churchill's watch only a few short years later, in 1951. Winston Churchill was also a freemason. Prior to World War II, ethnicity and paganism went hand in hand, and had done for millennia. In 1945, Gardner made his way to London "intent on propagating his religion," which was a cobbled together mish-mash that confuses Teutonic and Celtic cultures but ultimately leads practitioners away from both. While there is no smoking gun to prove a conspiracy, these are interesting coincidences to take note of.

European Animism

We can see that Europeans once had an animistic worldview just like other indigenous spiritual systems, that this was distinctly ethnic-based, but this did not equate modern liberal "we are one" nonsense – at least not until 1945. So, what did we believe and why does it behoove us to look to our own ethnic folkways in the modern world? Well, a good place to start is with the original meaning of the word "god." The early Judeo-Christian missionaries used cultural appropriation quite liberally when packaging their ideology to Europeans. Many words from our own indigenous lexicon were used to sell Christianity. The word "god" is only one of many words taken and twisted from its original meaning. It is a Teutonic origin word, with close cognates found all across the Germanic language landscape. Etymonoline says:

From Proto-Germanic *guthan (source also of Old Saxon, Old Frisian, Dutch god, Old High German got, German Gott, Old Norse guð, Gothic guþ)... perhaps from PIE *ghut- "that which is invoked" (source also of Old Church Slavonic zovo "to call," Sanskrit huta- "invoked," an epithet of Indra), from root *gheu(e)- "to call, invoke." The notion could be "divine entity summoned to a sacrifice."

But some trace it to PIE *ghu-to- "poured," from root *gheu- "to pour, pour a libation" (source of Greek khein "to pour," also in the phrase khute gaia "poured earth," referring to a burial mound. "Given the Greek facts, the Germanic form may have referred in the first instance to the spirit immanent in a burial mound.

Originally a neuter noun in Germanic, the gender shifted to masculine after the coming of

Christianity. Old English god probably was closer in sense to Latin numen."

So if the Teutonic word "god" was closer to the Latin word *"numen,"* what is the meaning of *numen*? Per Merrium-Webster, "numen: a spiritual force or influence often identified with a natural object, phenomenon, or place." Therefore, in the Germanic context, "god" had an animistic meaning. We believed that our landscape and the creatures within it were imbued with spiritual forces that we called gods. And the act of honoring these gods involved pouring libations, or offerings, in propitiation. This act also appealed to these spirits to invoke their presence. We offered sacrifice so that the gods might intercede here on Midgard. It is documented that sacred springs were venerated across European language boundaries. Dr. Brian Bates discusses the enchanted landscape of Northern Europeans in his book "The Real Middle Earth; Magic and Mystery in the Dark Ages." He draws a distinction between the more rationalist worldview of the Romans compared to that of the Celts and Teutons. However, he does have to concede some spiritual practices were held in common. He says,

"The Romans are counterpointed elsewhere in this book as lacking some of the imaginative sensitivities of Middle-earth culture. However, they also honored wells. One well dating back to prehistoric times was rediscovered in 1876. Excavations showed that it had originally been built by the Celts and had subsequently been taken over by the occupying Romans. Displacing the indigenous Celts, or at least setting up military overlordship, they built a fort at the well right at the northern border of England, called Brocolita, now named Carrawbrough. Artefacts recovered at the well show that it was dedicated to Coventina, almost certainly a local Celtic goddess who was adopted by the Romans," (Bates, 131).

But we know that the sacred wells and springs were honored in Britain even prior to the arrival of the Celts. A British documentary television series called "Walking Through History" hosted by Tony Robinson features an episode called "The Path to Stonehenge" which gives a lovely discussion with several leading anthropologists and historians about recent (as of 2013) theories regarding the purpose of Neolithic sites in Britain. Ancestor veneration features prominently in Neolithic European culture. But, water veneration also appears frequently. Robinson speaks with experts who explain the role of ancestors as guardians of the living, but also that water is venerated for its life-giving force. The official website for Stonehenge echoes this interpretation. Discussing the wider "complex" connecting Stonehenge to Avebury and Silbury Hill, the website says:

"In late winter/early spring, the winterbourne (dry in winter) river Kennet resurfaces and floods the low lying land,

The ditch surrounding Silbury Hill is filled and, again, forms the shape of the squatting Mother Goddess. Such a clever design, using the seasonal flow of the river to venerate the Provider and where, from the summit, She would be visible. The annual, fresh flow of life-giving water from the Swallowhead Spring to swell the River Kennet, would have held great significance to the populace living in and around Avebury. Swallowhead Spring, would have been seen as part of the Goddess's living body. We see Spring, the Herald of new life, the first Age of Man and the first Season of Mother Earth. Contrast the absence of the water flowing from the earth which could signify drought, crop failure and to those reliant on those waters, death if the Provider withheld the bounty."

Artwork by Arthur John

The Frankish Question

It is interesting that Bates discusses the Roman adoption of Celtic sacred springs, because Roman Christianity used the same tactic. Places that were seen as holy since time immemorial continued to be venerated by the populace even after nominal conversion. The historical record has preserved numerous edicts and letters of instruction from the Catholic hierarchy sometimes urging the destruction of indigenous European holy sites, the outlawing of veneration of natural objects, or sometimes instructions to appropriate these sites for Christian use. Della Hooke, in her well-researched book called "Trees in Anglo-Saxon England," gives a lengthy discussion citing ample historical documentation of the Christian attack on nature veneration. She says,

"Frankish [Christian] kings were anxious to wipe out the worship of springs, trees and sacred groves, and set fines in the later eighth century for those who thus made vows at such places or squandered praises on pagan gods and ordered that such trees, stones and springs where foolish lights or other observances were used or carried out should be removed or destroyed. The Council of Nantes in 895 specifically ordered the destruction of trees consecrated to 'demons' or local gods."

Interestingly, the Frankish attacks on indigenous European culture are further evidence that Rabbi Rosenzweig is accurate in his assertion regarding the relationship between Judaism and Christianity in their unity against the ethnikos, or pagans. A Jewish scholar called Arthur J. Zuckerman put intensive research into his book, "A Jewish Princedom in Feudal France, 768-900," published by Columbia University Press in 1972. Apparently, there was a Jewish principality in southern France that has been generally forgotten today. This community played a role in the story of Europe versus the Moors in Spain, in the early medieval trade routes, the establishment of networks of credit and the banking system, and also in the Christianization of Northern Europeans. According to Zuckerman's research, the Franks granted land to the Jews of Septimania on the condition that they locate a descendant of Israel's King David to crown as their own king. A scholar from the line of David was found in Babylonia and made king of Septimania. Author Lee Levin sums up the story in his article for "The Jewish Magazin" called "The Jewish Kingdom of Septimania," wherein he explains that the Carolingian dynasty lacked a royal bloodline and so their family married in with this new "King Machir". Levin says:

"[Machir] would give oaths of allegiance to the King of the Franks. King Charles requested that Machir marry his aunt Alda. A request from the King of the Franks was a command.

All now came clear. So this was why Pepin had required that the King of Septimania be a direct descendant of King David! The problem for Pepin, and for his son, King Charles, was that Pepin had usurped the throne of the Franks from the Merovingians, and thus there was no royal blood in their veins. This they desperately needed in order to establish the legitimacy of their dynasty. By this marriage of Alda to Machir,

who was a direct lineal descendant of King David, they would not only have royal blood in the veins of their descendants, but the most royal blood possible, the blood of David himself!

But how could such a marriage take place? Alda was Catholic, and no Catholic priest would marry her to a Jew unless the Jew converted, which of course Machir absolutely could not do. On the other hand, no rabbi would marry Machir to a gentile unless she converted. An unsolvable dilemma? Apparently not, for marry they did, and had a legitimate son through whom Jewish blood now was intermingled with that of the Carolingian kings of France."

It is further explained in Zuckerman's scholarly work that *"At the time Pepin admitted Makir to the high Frank aristocracy he may well have dubbed him with a distinguished dynastic name. Theodoric suggests itself because of its frequent reappearance in later generations of the Makhiri,"* (p212). Zuckerman asserts that the *"prevailing view that the Franks allied with the Goths defies the evidence. Pepin was* allied with Caliph of Bagdad and they worked together for a "Franco-'Abbasid domination over Spain," (p173). He continues,

"*After the fall of Narbonne and the amicable outcome of the negotiations the negotiations with Bagdad in 765-68, Pepin and his sons Carloman and Charles redeemed their pledge to the Jews, settled a scholar-prince in Narbonne by the name of Makhir, dubbed him Theodoric, gave him a Carolingian princess as wife, and endowed him with noble status in addition to vast allodial estates," (p173).*

(As an aside, that the Carolingian kings would bestow the name "Theodoric" upon this Davidic-line Jewish king is significant. The name contains the Germanic elements "theo," cognate to "deus," and ric/rik which means ruler).

That Pepin's son Charlemagne granted economic privileges to Jews in his realm is well supported in the historical record. The same is noted of Charlemagne's son, Louis the Pious. Charlemagne would go on to become famous for the horrific slaughter at Verdon, where he killed 4,500 unarmed Saxon chieftains in cold blood. Louis the Pious is thus named for his penchant for collecting all known writings on indigenous European culture and setting them alight.

These tactics would he echoed by converted Christian kings for centuries as they joined "Christendom," a forerunner to the modern E.U., which granted economic privileges and trade incentives. But, dedication to and practice of our indigenous folkways lingered on amongst the populace despite the efforts of

Artwork by Merry-Joseph Blondel

their elite overlords. Eventually, the Protestant Reformation would rightly notice that under Catholicism Europeans remained essentially pagan. And so, again, secular and religious authorities rounded up individuals suspected of engaging in their own indigenous practices and set living people on fire for this sin. That famous "Protestant work ethic" coincided with the rise of the mercantile economy and the capitalist machine that has dominated the West in more recent generations. While atheism is often blamed for the loss of the sacred, industrialization occurred in Western nations that were still overwhelmingly Christian. Industrialization arguably raped and abused the natural landscape both by unethical harvesting of resources and the pollution that ensued.

Moving Forward

Today we stand upon a precipice and ask ourselves "which way Western man?" Many are observant enough to see that those who present history are re-writing it in front of our very eyes. We can see media misrepresenting facts such as the historical ethnic demographics in Europe. That our academic and educational institutions are literally indoctrinating students from their tender years through university is news to no one. Yet, there is a chasm of disconnect when it comes to looking critically at the recording and telling of other areas of history and the roles that elite-imposed ideological pre-cursors to modern liberalism have played in driving us to the scenario in which we find ourselves today. The dissident right looks at the media and scoffs at the "lying press," while they simultaneously allow themselves to be manipulated by it. An analytic jaunt through the history of historical paganism, the figures responsible for spreading Christianity at sword point and their other connections and activities, coupled with a closer look at 20th century history turns the standard understanding on its head.

Shamanism, spiritualism, energy work, rainbows and crystals, totems and spirit animals belong to lefty wingnuts only so long as we eschew our own ethnic spiritual inheritance. This is a question of dire significance. For, when the fight for ethnic viability is over, immediate questions arise on the horizon. Will we defeat the globalists only to allow their goals to continue under the guise of universalism? But, more pressing will become the need to wrestle environmentalism away from the left. What good will it be to save our race if we have destroyed our own planet?

While it may not be realistic to expect a mass return to animism as a religion in the immediate, it can be said that had we never been forced to abandon the gods of our landscape we would have been better stewards of the Earth.

Western man must ask himself, squarely, if he believes in blood and soil. If the answer is yes, then hope springs eternal.

Bibliography:

Bates, Brian. The Real Middle Earth. Oxford: Sidgwick& Jackson, 2002.

Etymonline.com. God. n.d. 22 12 2012. <https://www.etymonline.com/word/god#etymonline_v_9016>.

Hooke, Della. Trees in Anglo-Saxon England. Woodbridge: The Boydell Press, 2010.

Levin, Lee. "The Messiah of Septimania." 2011. The Jewish Magazine. web. 22 12 2018. <http://www.jewishmag.com/175magSpengler. "Christian, Muslim, Jew: Frank Rosenzweig and the Abrahamic Religions." October 2007. First Things. web. 22 December 2018. <https://www.firstthings.com/article/2007/10/003-christian-muslim-jew>.

Stonehenge.co.uk. "Thoughts on its purpose." n.d. Stonehenge.co.uk. web. <http://www.stonehenge.co.uk/aveburythoughts.php>.

Walking Through History, Series 2, Episode 1. Perf. Tony Robinson. 2013. Television.

Wikipedia. Gerald Gardner (Wiccan). n.d. web. 22 12 2018. <https://en.wikipedia.org/wiki/Gerald_Gardner_(Wiccan)>.

Zuckerman, Arthur J. A Jewish princedom in feudal France, 768-900. New York: Columbia University Press, 1972.

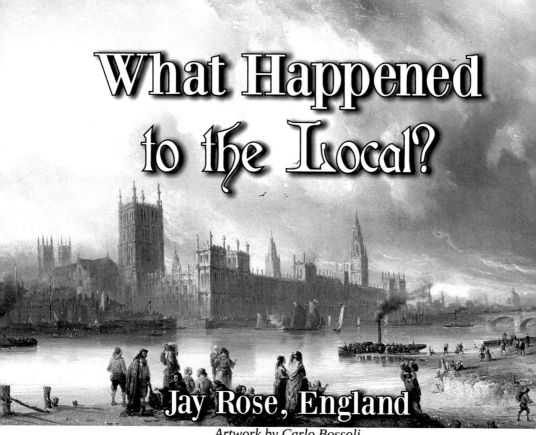

What Happened to the Local?

Jay Rose, England

Artwork by Carlo Bossoli

Ask someone to name a well-known English community that exists, (or at least did exist within living memory,) and someone is bound to mention the Cockneys, from whom I am partially descended. My Grandad was a true Cockney, born in ear-shot of the Bow Bells, but visit London today and you'll be hard pressed to find a white face at all. I often lament the fact that my family originally came from the East End of London, who among other reasons, left the capital to escape the immigrant influx not long after the Second World War. As a result, my family, like a great number of other ex-Londoners, left the capital to start a new life in the nearby county of Essex.

An interesting thing to note, though, is that whilst you might presume that the England of the nineteen-sixties was completely homogeneous, there still existed huge variations in the indigenous local cultures and language which sadly, like the Cockneys, have now almost completely disappeared. Fast forward to 2019 and the leafy suburbs and furrowed, flat fields of rural Essex have rapidly begun to resemble London's overspill. Overpopulation and over-development are quickly destroying any remaining agrarian charm that still existed around the town that I grew up in. Recognizing the fact that my area is fast becoming yet another "diverse" concrete jungle, I started documenting my area's history for posterity before it's gone forever - but that research has left me feeling a little somber.

I often forlorn the passing of white London, evidenced whenever you go anywhere near the capital. But, as I began over the last few years to read about local Essex history, something strange became apparent to me. "White flight" might not be *as* damaging, but it seems mass-immigration has had a negative compound affect as those who were pushed out of inner-cities by migration have inadvertently destroyed the local English communities that they moved into. It's hard to imagine today, but Essex was once far

removed from the county's current stereotype of white stilettos and fake tans. It was once known for its fruit farms, cattle, and superstitious belief in witchcraft. The dialect was also completely different from the "Estuary English" I am myself afflicted with. The accent in these parts was originally very rural, and sounded very similar to the surviving Suffolk and Norfolk accents. The local language itself also held on to some frankly bizarre localisms and remnants of Old English or Proto-Germanic words.

Sometimes, though, you come across something which challenges your core beliefs and that happened to me not too long ago whilst rummaging around the local library. I found a book entitled "Essex Survivals" written by Fred Roe and in it he gives a personal account of his experiences with members of a rural community in the village of Heybridge. Reading these stories today, they seem rather comical. But, I think they highlight just how far removed our sense of community has sunk to today. In one personal account, Roe tells the story of just how cohesive local communities once were, and how much animosity they had against outsiders. Whilst I don't think that is something we should seek to emulate, we should at least bare it in mind:

"...against the walls of the 'Ship' Inn, at the lock gates, were some forms, and here congregated the usual knot of gossipers from the adjoining cottages. The sunset was deepening into a succession of ravishing colours as a tall man strode up the incline and stopped in front of the merry-makers. I can see the man now, a well-built fellow of the labouring class, fustian clad, and with a ragged tawny moustache descending in Viking fashion over his lower jaw. His boots were white with dust from the roads, and slung over his shoulder was a rush satchel. A typical East Anglian, with not a bad face, and a tired manner.

Conversation instantly ceased, and the Heybridge group looked blankly at the new arrival.

'Evenin', mates, he ventured.

'Evenin',' came the very distant response.

'Warmer than ever,' continued the new-comer.

'That's so.'

'I be going up to Stubbing's,' volunteered the tall man.

'Ay.'

The man did not sit down, but leaned down on the stout stick he was carrying as though fatigued. Obviously he was not wanted. The sunset was on his face and I noticed his eyes were bright blue. There was a curiously pensive look about him, as if wishful for companionship. In another class of life he would have been a dreamer.

Not another word would the cronies vouchsafe but impenetrable monosyllables. The tall man finished his modest half-measure of ale, and bidding the others good night strode off towards Maldon through the light mist which was already rising from the canal.

'They seemed to treat that man pretty coolly,' I remarked to an onlooker.

'Like as not,' was the reply; 'whoy, he's a foreigner.'

'A foreigner,' I queried; 'he looked British enough.'

'That may be, but he's a foreigner.'

'He seemed a decent sort of fellow.'

'Very like, but a foreigner. And we don't hold with suchlike. He comes from Goldhanger.'

Goldhanger being some four or five miles away. The unwelcome intruder having departed, conversation and laughter recommenced."

It seems remarkable that just a hundred years ago the local communities in England were still so small that they considered the next village along as a foreign entity. Compare this with today, where few know or even care to know their next door neighbours anymore. And perhaps it should be of no surprise that there seems an underlying sense of indifference and apathy regarding a lack of immediate local or even national identity. That sense of belonging is, or at least was, an integral part of what makes us human, and missing that component of "us and them" in our lives may well be why so many people in this age are rendered nothing more than semi-suicidal consumers.

The current situation with the way the world is as a whole has disenfranchised and isolated individuals more than make them feel part of some universal collective. Not only that, but with us all being forced

Artwork by Frederick Brown

by law to consider everyone, regardless of their background, a member of our own communities, it has destroyed any chance of groups forming organically of their own accord. It seems as though this model for society is great only at increasing economic output by effectively demoralising everyone to the point where the only thing left to live for is the pursuit of material items. Criminalising this innate desire to create an 'us' is perhaps the reason why today we're seeing so many different political or identity problems in the West. I'm not suggesting that we start ignoring people who happen to live in the next town or village, but what I do think is that it's rather important for us to get back some sort of local cohesion, whether that be at a parish level or a wider area.

Of course it's important to remember that the mind-set a hundred years ago, as it is today, is very much dependent on a sense of geography. Whilst trains and trams had begun to improve transport links for main towns and cities by the early twentieth century, most rural communities still had to rely predominately on horse and cart. It seems strange to us today, but most villagers hardly ever left the town or village that they happened to be born in. Another interesting account from Fred Roe's book, describes in some detail what the rural folk considered far-off travelling at that time:

"There was a picturesque old hand who pottered about the inn doing odd jobs, and after receiving several small tips for allowing me to sketch his rugged face 'Owd Charley' opened himself up to me.

'Yes, you're a foreigner here, sure, but you're no' a bad 'un,' he sagely observed. He told me his age and with great pride, adding with emphasis, 'I've been a traveller in my time.'

'That is interesting,' I remarked; 'the folks round here don't seem to travel about much.'

'No, not they,' replied Owd Charley. 'Why, Mrs ----- is getting on for eighty an' she's never been to Brentwood. No, nor even to Ingatestone either. But I've been a traveller, I have.'

'Have you crossed over to France?'

'France! No,' - the old man spat contemptuously into a

ditch,--' but I've been as far as Suffolk, I have. Twice I've been to Suffolk.'

I pondered upon the vastness of such an enterprise. The nearest point of Suffolk is close to thirty miles distant. 'Owd Charley' took my silence for admiration..."

It seems laughable today, but to someone who could only travel thirty or so miles by foot or on the back of some old nag, you're realistically looking at a two or three day journey. To our modern perspectives who are used to mass transit, two or three days of travel via car could get you from England to Italy – so the difference in worldview is perhaps understandable.

And yes, the modern age has brought with it tremendous luxuries that even decades ago were considered to be the preserve of royalty. But luxuries are just that. They are a treat. A perk. The unfortunate thing is that in opening up our world to all these luxuries, we have made our planet smaller and destroyed something important; our community and our sense of belonging. It's not enough to consider yourself a "citizen of the world" which is an empty phrase and does nothing except emphasize how rootless and empty somebody is.

The point I'm trying to make with this article is a simple one, albeit verging on revolutionary given today's state of affairs. Europe, along with the rest of the world as a whole, has lost so much of its original culture and true diversity in terms of folk traditions, language and (dare I say it) demographics, and it really is a terrible shame. Part of this has been caused by multiculturalism, but that itself is only a single facet within globalism which has the overall agenda to strip this world into a boring, uniform, Borg-like collective. We must recognise the extensive damage that has been done to us all so far, and work together to try and preserve all on this planet in the name of true diversity - and not the newspeak version that has come to replace it.

Most of the nationalists or pro-European movements today, like the Alt-Right, seem to want to unite around the idea of saving Europe or "the white race" as a single unified entity against the threats that we all collectively face. Whilst on one level I agree with this sentiment wholeheartedly, there is perhaps a more important layer to this struggle that few in nationalist circles ever address. Our tools as human beings never evolved to give a damn about people outside of our own tribe, and by tribe in this sense, I specifically refer to the theory in psychology referred to as "Dunbar's Number" that puts a limit on the number of other people you are able to have decent relationships with at any given time.

My argument would be that the apathy Europe and much of the wider world seems to be stuck in at the moment is not due our people not feeling "European" enough. As time has gone by even those of us in Britain who voted for Brexit have felt more and more kinship with our continental brethren - but I strongly suspect that the rampant apathy across Europe and further afield is caused more by a complete lack of local identity, rather than a continental or racially based one. Until people are able to network in real life and actually gain a sense of belonging to those closest around them, apathy even among those who are "red-pilled" will continue to be a major issue in any anti-globalist, or anti-universalist movement.

Without a weakening of local community, do you really think that the abuse of women and children at the hands of foreigners would continue? Would cohesive local

Artwork by Myles Birket Foster

communities allow the building of refugee centres in their towns? Or the building of foreign religious places of worship? If people knew that the immediate community had their backs, even if the state didn't, none of these problems would be happening without considerable local backlash. Meanwhile, although I too am guilty for this, most of us "red pilled" folk are too busy chatting to people hundreds of miles away over the internet, pacified by the act of talking about how bad things are and how terrible we feel - instead of acting constructively.

So my (perhaps not so) revolutionary solution to the problem in Europe in the face of globalism and multiculturalism is recognizing that whilst internet networking is great, it is by no means a substitute for creating real local communities or at the very least, keeping local culture alive by talking about it and sharing it with others out there. Individually we have very little power, but we can at the very least try and keep our own backyards in shape as we await a chance at something grander. There are hundreds of things that we could all do locally that would end up more meaningful than constantly circle-jerking online. And the best thing about all this is that networking in the real world is a good excuse for meeting down the local pub to complain about foreigners.

Artwork by Henry Dawson

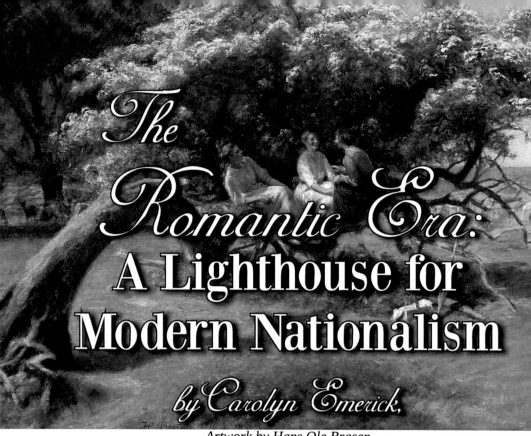

The Romantic Era: A Lighthouse for Modern Nationalism

by Carolyn Emerick,

Artwork by Hans Ole Brasen

Nineteenth and twentieth century nationalism did not arise in a vacuum. Indeed, the massive political gains that nationalists succeeded in securing were instigated and buoyed by prior and concurrent cultural movements. We see a populist revival in political nationalist sentiment across the West today, but, although there has been a great deal of commentary on the decline in our cultural output in recent decades, there has been very little discussion on cultural revival. Moreover, while there has been public shock and outrage at the demonization of our ethnic heritage, there has been little widespread interest in Western history as a subject. A phrase that I have been using with ever more frequency is: the past is a lighthouse, we must let it illuminate our present as we build our future. At this juncture, a time when we are awakening en masse to the hijacking of Western society and postulating what can be done to change our cultural trajectory, it behooves us to look more closely at a period in our own history that bears many analogies to the situation in which we find ourselves today. I am speaking of the Romantic Era.

The Romantic Movement has been largely considered a literary and artistic movement. This view falls short, however, for several reasons. The first reason being that scholars note that there is not one overriding style that pervades Romantic Era art, unlike other artistic movements. The Romantic Movement is better said to be more of a feeling, or a zeitgeist, that electrified artistic creators and appreciators of their creations. As is noted frequently, this feeling was profoundly spiritual. However, an important theme underpinning the Romantic Era that has been virtually ignored by modern academia is that this shared feeling was profoundly ethnic. To understand how the Romantic Movement arose and what its meaning was, we must look first to the preceding Age of Enlightenment, for here is where we find the fodder for the reactionary movement which would follow it.

The Enlightenment saw the birth of the field of science as a mainstream discipline. But, with that, it also ushered in a sterilized worldview. There is often a tendency, mainly found among American Evangelicals, to view previous eras as profoundly pious and steeped in Christian dogma. In reality, most of the great thinkers of the 18th century were Deists. They believed in a creator, to be sure, but just as a master watchmaker puts the gears in motion and then set the timepiece loose to function independently, the world was operationally mechanized. So pervasive was this outlook that even the likes of Thomas Jefferson set out to "correct" the New Testament by re-writing it as he thought it must have actually happened – removing all supernatural elements from the narrative. The mechanized view of the world would only become more intense with the onset of the Industrial Revolution in the first half of the 19th century. Now, not only was a mechanized world a philosophical view, but it was quickly becoming a literal reality. This swift technological transformation was cause for alarm for many. There was a real fear about where this new mechanical world would lead us; as evidenced in Mary

Shelley's famous novel, "Frankenstein; or, The Modern Prometheus," which is not actually a gothic horror story about a monster so much as an observation and stark warning for mankind about moving so quickly toward a scientific worldview that removed the soul from humanity.

While industrialization brought with it undeniable benefits, it also brought vast and sweeping changes to both the landscape and to lifestyles which, in many cases, could be a shock to the system. The populist nationalism that we see rising today has rightly noted the repercussions of the phenomenon that has been coined "globalism" in our current epoch. It is fair to say that the Industrial Age could be considered "Globalism 1.0." While there had been periods of mass shifts in populations previously (tribal migrations, and more recently the settling of European colonies), industrialization ramped up population shifts concurrently with lifestyle changes that had been hitherto unfathomable in the history of mankind. One notable difference was that whereas historically, most mass movements of people occurred together in tribal or otherwise ethnic groups, this new occurrence saw movement undertaken by the individual. However, when individuals are moving in massively large numbers, this can have a striking impact on place.

Of course, this mass movement of individuals coincided with the process of urbanization, wherein people who had hitherto lived bonded to their locale for generations were suddenly uprooted due to the need to seek wage work in the boom cities. We are

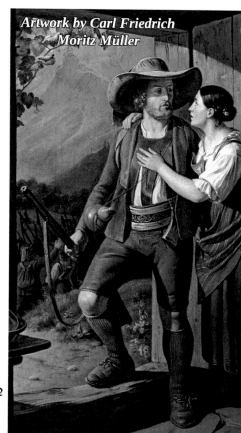

Artwork by Carl Friedrich Moritz Müller

culturally still quite familiar with the squalid conditions in 19th century Western urban centers thanks to the work of Charles Dickens. But, what many modern readers may not fully realize is the impact that the combined efforts of the Enlightenment (or, Age of Reason/Science) plus industrialization resulting in urbanization had on Europeans culturally. This is where the Romantics enter the picture. Like those who are awakening to a racial awareness across the West today, the Romantics looked and saw their world changing in ways that were not for the better. Individuals who moved to urban centers lost their bond to the soil, but more than that, to their kinfolk. Of course, cities with large numbers of immigrants from the same regions developed ghettos wherein they thrived for a time in their own ethnic-enclaves (the many "Little Italy" or "China Town" neighborhoods found in large American cities are a testament to the natural desire for people to live among their own kind). But, within a generation or two, descendants of the initial migrating people soon lose the ethnic bonds that their ancestors once possessed.

However, the main point of concern of the Romantics was the other side of the coin – the impact that the outflow of population had on the cultural viability of the people left behind.

Today we see a massive influx of people from the Third World into Western nations. While nationalists are rightly noting the effect that this influx of foreigners has on our societies, it is also noted by patriots in their own home countries that the outflow of educated individuals results in a phenomenon known as "brain drain." Whereas, modern "brain drain" is defined as the impact that the exodus of a nation's most educated citizens has upon that society, an analogous phenomenon occurred in the rural communities of Europe when their young folk left in great numbers to relocate to urban centers or even to emigrate to the New World. In the case of 19th century Europe, it was not necessarily highly skilled people who were leaving, but it was simply the "folk" themselves. Therefore, this "brain drain" resulted in more of a cultural drain. These were not doctors, engineers, and scientists leaving their home nations without high-tier minds. They were simply farm hands and regular country folk. But, these people were far more valuable than highly educated doctors, engineers, and scientists in terms of the innate knowledge that they carried from generation to generation of their own folk culture. When these people vacated their homelands in large numbers, the impact upon the folk tradition of Europe was palpable.

It was not only the unsettling shift to an overly rationalist and mechanized view of the world, but also the realization that something of immense value was being lost that birthed the Romantic Movement. This was not some "romanticized" view of backbreaking manual farm labor that the Romantics were concerned with; but rather, they were concerned with the spirit and the soul of the folk which had been preserved through all those generations before mechanized farming machinery started to make laborers redundant. These were people who had passed down stories steeped in ethnic spiritual tradition for, in some cases, literally thousands of years. These were people who sang songs handed down from their grandparents' grandparents, regaling ever new crops of younger generations with tales of heroes of their ancestral past. These were people who passed down holiday customs and traditions that can only be described as ritual remnants of a

Artwork by Arthur Hughes

past so ancient that it is not found in any historical source. And these were the people vacating their lands to lose themselves in the city. A recognition permeated the middle class educated demographic, and thank the good gods that it did, that something immensely important to themselves (and to all of us, even today) was about to be lost. Something had to be done about it.

So, again, rather than an artistic movement per se, what defines the Romantic Movement is this deeply spiritual drive to reach into the folk-soul of ethnic European cultural inheritance. The European folk-soul was not only a muse for some of the most beautiful works of art, music, poetry, and literature ever produced in the Western tradition during this era, but there was also an intellectual understanding of the need to protect and preserve our indigenous culture. So, while the Pre-Raphaelite Brotherhood in England was painting visual artworks inspired by European myths, legends, and history, Walter Scot in Scotland was writing epic historical fiction novels of adventure about our glorious past. But, likewise, the likes of Robert Burns recognized the value in regional dialect and made an effort to create poetic works of linguistic beauty in the Scots language (rather than using the standard English of the educated classes). And, perhaps, most important while simultaneously unrecognized and undervalued is that the Romantic Era saw the birth of the field of folklore as a discipline far and wide from Britain to Russia. It was in German speaking regions where the field of folklore has been most remembered, through the efforts of Jacob and Wilhelm Grimm.

While there had been individuals recording the lore of the people prior to the 19th century, there was never a widespread effort or a name applied to the subject, and it was during this period that the term "folk-lore" was coined. It cannot be overemphasized the emphatic importance and depth of meaning in this term. Folklore, as a genre, has been neglected and downplayed as sort of quaint, lowbrow babble of the peasantry. High literature which is the brain-child of geniuses like Shakespeare,

Milton, and the greats of the Western literary cannon has received its rightful praise over the years. But, the lore of the folk has been relegated to the realm of children's stories. Which, in and of itself, in my view, is a testament to its deeply embedded subconscious meaning and value rather than any negative connotation. It should be considered that when it comes time to read stories to our wee ones, what do we choose? Sure there are many modern classics of children's literature, but we have never strayed from the European folk and fairytale canon. On a psychological level, it speaks volumes that these are the stories that we make sure to pass on with each subsequent generation – the lore of our own folk.

That these tales are, indeed, the lore of our own folk should not be glossed over. As academia has moved ever to the left, which in the West actually means ethno-masochism, there has been a drive to separate the field of folklore from its origins in the space where the Romantic Era bleeds into the rise of ethno-nationalism. For, circling back to the beginning, nothing exists in a vacuum. The nationalist movements in Europe did not arise out of some anomaly in space-time. The people of Europe saw not only their own lives, but their wider societies, and the very landscapes that surrounded them changing dramatically before their very eyes. And, of course, there was a natural reaction to this. The Romantic Movement extended more or less over a one hundred year period, with its peak typically defined as about 1850-1900. If we look to European nationalism, there is a stark overlap with the rise and advancements of European nationalist movements riding on the heels of the drive for cultural preservation fomented by the Romantic Movement. Mainstream academics today attempt to universalize folklore and separate it from ethnic nationalism. In truth, nothing could be a more egregious degradation of the field which owes its very birth to the recognition of the importance of preserving that which belongs to our own folk. Within the folk tradition is preserved the kernels of cultural identity which grow and blossom in the great flourishings of cultural expression that the Western artistic tradition has produced in an unbroken line dating to the Classical Era.

Just as misplaced, however, is the attempt to elicit political nationalism without a grounding in these ethno-cultural foundations. While the populist nationalist awakening seen widespread across the West is to be applauded, we must also take caution. Never in the history of mankind has any culture of substance been built without a grounding in its own ethnic past. The contemporary nationalist movement of our current age is fueled by reactionary response to attacks by forces we generalize as "globalists." It is good and right that we are recognizing these attacks and reacting to them with a nationalistic response. But, if we are to take this energy and use it to build a society upon which we can stand firmly for many generations to come, we must build our foundations firmly on the inheritance that we have received from the countless generations who have come before us, our own folk. The past is a lighthouse; let it illuminate our present as we build our future.

Artwork by Hans Ole Brasen

28595404R00049

Made in the USA
San Bernardino, CA
07 March 2019